VOLUME 5

THE COLLECTED WORKS OF ARTHUR SELDON

Government Failure and Over-Government

THE COLLECTED WORKS OF ARTHUR SELDON

VOLUME 1	The Virtues of Capitalism
VOLUME 2	The State Is Rolling Back
VOLUME 3	Everyman's Dictionary of Economics
VOLUME 4	Introducing Market Forces into "Public" Services
VOLUME 5	Government Failure and Over-Government
VOLUME 6	The Welfare State: Pensions, Health, and Education
VOLUME 7	The IEA, the LSE, and the Influence of Ideas (includes an index to the series)

Arthur Seldon

VOLUME 5

THE COLLECTED WORKS OF ARTHUR SELDON

Government Failure and Over-Government

ARTHUR SELDON

Edited and with a New Introduction by Colin Robinson

LIBERTY FUND, Indianapolis

This book is published by Liberty Fund, Inc., a foundation established to encourage study of the ideal of a society of free and responsible individuals.

The cuneiform inscription that serves as our logo and as the design motif for our endpapers is the earliest-known written appearance of the word "freedom" (*amagi*), or "liberty." It is taken from a clay document written about 2300 B.C. in the Sumerian city-state of Lagash.

Printed in the United States of America
09 08 07 06 05 C 5 4 3 2 1
09 08 07 06 05 P 5 4 3 2 1

Library of Congress Cataloging-in-Publication Data
Seldon, Arthur.
Government failure and over-government / Arthur Seldon; edited and with a new introduction by Colin Robinson.
p. cm.—(The collected works of Arthur Seldon; v. 5)
Includes bibliographical references and index.
Contents: Introduction—Change by degree or by convulsion—Individual liberty, public goods, and representative democracy—Avoision—The dilemma of democracy—Public choice in Britain—On the liberal emancipation of mankind.
ISBN 0-86597-546-9 (hard cover: alk. paper)—ISBN 0-86597-554-X (pbk.: alk. paper)
1. Democracy. 2. Welfare state. 3. Liberty. 4. Public goods. 5. Liberalism. 6. Social choice—Great Britain. 7. Great Britain—Politics and government—1979–1997. 8. Great Britain—Politics and government—1997– . I. Robinson, Colin, 1932– . II. Title.

JC423 .S433 2005
321.8—dc22

2004064927

LIBERTY FUND, INC.
8335 Allison Pointe Trail, Suite 300
Indianapolis, Indiana 46250-1684

CONTENTS

INTRODUCTION

Six works are featured in volume 5 of The Collected Works of Arthur Seldon. They are on a theme to which his writing constantly returns—the problem of over-government.

In representative democracies, such as the United States and the United Kingdom, governments claim legitimacy from their election by a majority (or a plurality) of the citizens of the country. Yet, once elected to office, usually on the broadest of policy platforms, they have a monopoly of policy making which leaves their actions largely unconstrained until the next election and sees them open to the influence of powerful interest groups that wish to obtain benefits for themselves at the expense of the rest of the community.

Seldon perceives serious dangers in the power of governments to coerce—for example, by taxing or by imposing regulations—which permits and indeed induces them to go beyond traditional functions of government (such as national defense, the maintenance of law and order, and the establishment and safeguarding of property rights). Governments plead the need to supply "public" goods and services, yet there is little "public" about much of their activity. Over-government is a constant threat and is very damaging: in Seldon's view, government failure is ubiquitous, both because governments have insufficient knowledge to identify and achieve "public interest" goals and because, even if they could determine what is the "public interest," they lack incentive to pursue it if it conflicts with their own aims. *Government Failure and Over-Government* contains two recent works on this subject—a book, *The Dilemma of Democracy*, published in 1998, and Seldon's section of another book, *Government: Whose Obedient Servant?*, written in 2000, to which Gordon Tullock and Gordon Brady contributed the other two sections. These two very substantial pieces are accompanied by three articles from the late 1970s and one from 2000.

The first paper, "Change by Degree or by Convulsion," written in 1978, is taken from an Institute of Economic Affairs (IEA) collection (*The Coming Confrontation: Will the Open Society Survive to 1989?*, Hobart Paperback 12, edited by Ralph Harris and Seldon). In the preface to the collection, Seldon argues that, though the idea of the market is (in the late 1970s) back in public discourse, politicians are still trying to suppress markets, moving toward a closed society. Harris and Seldon therefore asked a number of distinguished scholars, including Friedrich Hayek, for their views on how difficult it would be to reopen society. These scholars were sent a "preamble" which, in effect, asked them whether, when whole sections of society have been closed, they could be reopened by argument alone or whether some kind of revolution might be required.

In "Change by Degree or by Convulsion" Seldon argues that, in a market economy with decentralized decisions, change tends to be gradual and peaceful as adjustment takes place to changes in underlying supply-and-demand conditions. Confrontations are small and are "solved by higgling and haggling over price, the peace-maker" (p. 3). By contrast, in a centralized economy, change is repressed and postponed so that, when it comes, it is "contrived, jerky, discontinuous, lumpy, convulsive" (ibid.). Markets can deal peacefully with change; however, under government control, incipient economic change produces strife and tension and possibly even civil war where change is suppressed.

Seldon goes on to identify some of the sources of resistance to economic change in Britain in the late 1970s. Government legislation, going back a hundred years, has given legal privileges to the labor unions that, not surprisingly, they use to obstruct change. State ownership of the fuel and transport industries and state control of education and health also inhibit change and make the industries vulnerable to labor union pressure. The monopoly power of the state corporations allows high-wage costs to be passed on to consumers. Failure to alter the law on trade unions and to denationalize state monopolies risks a major confrontation. The open society, says Seldon, "cannot long survive a power created or tolerated by Parliament that is invited to bargain with government" (p. 5). "The longer the disarmament of the monopoly unions is shirked, the more painful it will have to be" (ibid.). Governments have brought this problem on themselves by their encroachments on what used to be the private sector, using the false claim that they are providing "public goods."

Yet, as usual, Seldon sees hope in growing resistance from the public to the interventions of the state. In the end, as Böhm-Bawerk foresaw, economic laws will prove stronger than political power. People will find their way back to the market.

> [T]he British, who have seen the market increasingly suppressed or repressed, and can now judge the results, will want to restore it—not least in medicine and education, where it was said to be least practicable. (p. 19)

Only a few years after Seldon wrote this, the Thatcher governments had, in the early 1980s, embarked on denationalization and a significant reduction in the legal privileges of trade unions, though it is only in very recent years that the first small steps toward markets in health and education have been taken in Britain.

The over-government theme continues in the second article in this volume, "Individual Liberty, Public Goods, and Representative Government: Lessons from the West and Escape for the East,"[1] originally published in 1979 in the German journal *ORDO.*

Seldon begins the article by quoting Hayek, including Hayek's contribution to *The Coming Confrontation* (see above), which stresses the dangers of majority rule and the threat from sectional interests that influence government. Seldon points out that the state has expanded remorselessly even though most of the arguments used to support the case for "free" government provision of services are false. Political choices are crude and arbitrary:

> if there is no market in which each man's pound or dollar, or Deutschmark, or franc is the same as everyone else's, access will be based on much more arbitrary differences in power, cultural or political, that are more difficult to correct or remove. (pp. 34–35)

Governments cannot accurately reflect public preferences: political majority decisions should be confined to genuine public goods.

One way of trying to reduce the size of government, says Seldon, is to impose cash limits on government departments. But a better approach is to use standard microeconomic principles, as he advocated in *Charge*[2]—to introduce prices for personal and private services supplied by governments so

1. A shortened version of this article appears under the title "Individual Liberty and Representative Democracy," in Seldon's *The State Is Rolling Back,* which is volume 2 of these Collected Works.

2. In volume 4 of these Collected Works.

that consumers can choose for themselves how much to purchase and therefore what the size of government should be.

Tax "avoision" is a word coined by Arthur Seldon to indicate the blurred distinction between the (legal) avoidance of tax and (illegal) evasion. The third article in this volume, "Avoision: The Moral Blurring of a Legal Distinction Without an Economic Difference," is his prologue to a symposium on tax avoision assembled by the IEA in 1979 (*Tax Avoision: The Economic, Legal and Moral Inter-Relationships Between Avoidance and Evasion,* IEA Readings 22). In the prologue he emphasizes that, on economic grounds, there is virtually no distinction between avoidance and evasion because their causes and their consequences are the same. Nor are there clear lessons to be drawn about the morality of those who evade tax or those who merely avoid it but nevertheless appear to defy the spirit of the law.

Avoidance and evasion have become so widespread, according to Seldon, that they conceal a considerable part of economic activity and make national statistics misleading. There is a trend to make payments in cash as part of a subterranean economy created in response to government rules and restrictions, and a large tax avoision industry has appeared that consumes the time and talents of many people.

Seldon makes another important point about taxes that is often ignored in public discussion. They are a very blunt instrument because of the difficulty of distinguishing their incidence from their impact. Governments may intend to tax a particular group (for example, "soaking the rich" or levying a tax on a specific industry), but where the tax eventually falls (its incidence) depends on price elasticities of demand. Because of the uncertainty about incidence, one of Adam Smith's "four canons of taxation" (certainty) can never be satisfied. Thus, "all taxation systems," says Seldon, are "precarious as instruments of government policy" (p. 66).

The fourth work in this volume, *The Dilemma of Democracy,* is best seen as a companion to *Capitalism.*[3] The latter explained the virtues of the capitalist system and the emptiness of the socialist critique, arguing at the same time that democratic governments had expanded their activities well beyond those that could be justified. In *The Dilemma of Democracy,* Seldon brings together and then expands the criticisms of democracy that are explicit or implicit in much of his earlier work, but particularly in *Capitalism.*

Democracy has failed, says Seldon. Lincoln's vision—government of the people, by the people, for the people—has not anywhere been fulfilled.

3. In volume 1 of these Collected Works.

> No democracy, certainly not in Britain, represents even indirect government of the people, the whole people, and nothing but the people. . . . No democratic government allows small groups of minorities to accept or reject its rules and regulations, laws and taxes, and to live as they wish, even where diversity to suit individuals, small groups and minorities is feasible. (pp. 88–89)

Majority rule has become the "source of arbitrary rule. Political democracy represents some of the people more than others" (p. 89).

Seldon uses the results of research by the public choice theorists to explain how over-government arises as members of governments pursue their own interests and are unduly swayed by the activities of interest groups that obtain privileges for their own members at the expense of the rest of the community. But, he points out, the power of government is not absolute. As it becomes bloated, so citizens seek to escape using markets. For example, rather than pay taxes they perceive to be excessive, they shift from the official economy to the "parallel economy" or they move to another country. As communications have improved, and especially as the Internet has developed, so has citizens' power of exit been enhanced.

In part 3 of *Dilemma,* Seldon analyzes this power of exit in some detail, in terms of a number of "escapes" that are open to citizens who regard government as excessive. He considers, for example, escape to the "parallel," or "shadow," economy, which is evidence of "widespread alienation from democratic government" (p. 126). Other "escapes" Seldon discusses are by barter, by electronic money, by the Internet (which much improves the discovery process of competitive markets), and to other countries (which can now be achieved without moving because of the expansion of free trade and improved communications).

Governments are powerful, concludes Seldon, but they are not as powerful as market forces. As he stressed in the first article in this volume, in the end political power must yield to the laws of economics. The dilemma of democracy has been provoked by the "new inability of government to maintain its supremacy over the market" (p. 146). Governments should realize that they would be well advised to retreat before they are rolled back anyway by the will of the people.

Seldon's view of the scale of that withdrawal is not merely some marginal reduction in the size of government. His agenda is much more radical—the state should halve its size relative to national income, shrinking from around 40 percent to nearer 20 percent.

"Public Choice in Britain," the fifth paper in this volume, is Seldon's contribution to *Government: Whose Obedient Servant? A Primer in Public Choice,* published in 2000 by the IEA as Readings 51, with coauthors Gordon Tullock and Gordon Brady.[4] The book had been conceived in the mid-1980s, when Seldon was still at the Institute of Economic Affairs but did not come to fruition until the late 1990s.

Tullock, Brady, and Seldon each wrote separate sections of the book, which, as its subtitle implies, is intended to set out the elements of public choice analysis for students and others interested in economic principles. Seldon's chapter follows an exposition of public choice analysis and its principal conclusions by Gordon Tullock, one of the founding fathers of public choice, and a discussion by Gordon Brady of some of the applications of the theory.

Seldon begins by explaining the problems inherent in collective choice when the decisions are made by representatives of the public rather than the public itself. As he says,

> The indirect results that emerge in the politically-decided production of goods and services are usually very different from those that would be chosen directly by the public itself. (p. 150)

The present "democratic" regime embodies a voting system that does not faithfully reflect voters' preferences, in which rent-seeking and log-rolling are endemic, and in which bureaucrats recommend policies that serve bureaucratic interests rather than the general public or the consumer. Hence government constantly expands, taxation is excessive, there is too much legislation, and "government persistently provides services which are clearly personal and family, though misleadingly described as 'public' or 'social'" (p. 154).

Choice is denied, and the state supplies mediocre, standardized services for which citizens are increasingly reluctant to pay, indirectly by taxes or directly by charges. Government, says Seldon, "has been inflated beyond its optimum limits. It should be decentralised and confined to its irreducible boundaries" (p. 155).

Seldon goes on to explain why the "welfare state," in particular, should be dismantled, allowing taxes to be reduced and permitting citizens to spend

4. A US edition of this book was published by the Cato Institute, Washington, D.C., in 2002, under the title *Government Failure: A Primer in Public Choice.*

their own money on goods and services they choose (rather than those chosen for them). There are three "crucial defects" in the state supply of "welfare" services. These services were introduced too soon, based on an ignorance of history and false arguments about the supposed superiority of state services; they became too large and failed to reflect individual preferences; and they were continued for too long after they had become superfluous because of the feasibility of private provision.

In his final chapter, "The Escapes from Over-Government," Seldon returns to one of the main themes of *The Dilemma of Democracy* (see above). As government becomes burdensome, people will find means to escape it: he gives as an example the way British parents are escaping from the inadequacies of state education to private schools or to private tutors for their children.

The Hobbesian choice—between government or anarchy—is false, says Seldon. The alternatives are not "government or no government but too little or too much government" (p. 189). In the twenty-first century, political power will have to be used "in deference to the sentiments of the populace who will have new powers to challenge the state." People will find "they can escape as they never could before" (p. 190).

The final article in the volume, "On the Liberal Emancipation of Mankind," is a brief paper from a festschrift for Christian Watrin, which was published in 2000 in the Friedrich A. von Hayek Institute's International Library of Austrian Economics series. The paper contains the essence of Seldon's views on the extent to which government has over-reached itself and on the escape mechanisms which people are employing.

He goes beyond his earlier papers in arguing that Böhm-Bawerk's question about the relative strengths of political power and economic law has been decisively answered in the 1990s. In a bold prediction, Seldon suggests that, in the first two decades of the twenty-first century, the growing escape from government will shrink the share of government in national income from 40 percent to not just 20 percent (as suggested in *The Dilemma of Democracy*) but to only 10 percent, both in North America and in Europe. "'Democratic' politicians have abused their powers to act as benefactors" (p. 195). State taxes are therefore "being rejected, its regulations bypassed, its rules flouted" (ibid.). The state is in retreat because of the superiority of the market.

The papers in this volume, covering a period of twenty-five years, show how Seldon's thought has developed into a more and more detailed critique of government action, especially when it involves "welfare" provision, leading him to foresee a radical reduction in the size of government as it cuts the functions it performs. According to Seldon, this reduction is inevitable because, if governments will not make the cuts voluntarily, they will be forced to do so by the actions of their citizens, who will increasingly escape through markets.

CHANGE BY DEGREE OR BY CONVULSION

Change by Degree or by Convulsion

The form in which change takes place, and therefore the intensity of the resistance to it, depends on its rate. Here is perhaps the most fundamental distinction between the market and government. In a functioning market with monopoly bottlenecks minimised and access to supply widened by topping up low incomes, decisions in adapting supply to demand are decentralised to individual undertakings or establishments—factories and shops, mines and docks, schools and hospitals. Change is organic, gradual, continuous, by degree. It affects relatively small numbers. Disturbance, dislocation, disruption are minimised. The "confrontations" in the market are small, and solved by higgling and haggling over price, the peace-maker.

In a state economy or state industries, decisions are centralised to planning boards, committees, commissions, councils, government departments, that nominally "represent" the very much larger number of workers, managers and consumers who will benefit or suffer. Change is therefore more likely to be opposed, repressed, inhibited, postponed. When it takes place it is contrived, jerky, discontinuous, lumpy, convulsive. Disturbance, dislocation, disruption are large-scale. Friction is inflated.

In a market there are therefore better prospects that change will be peaceful. In a government economy change is more likely to provoke tension, strife, and unrest, and, if it is suppressed, violence, bloodshed and civil war.

Since the end of World War II the British economy has become more and more resistant to change, and therefore more prone to discontinuous, "disruptive" change. The central government solidified the growing structure of variegated health services into "the" National Health Service, education into standardised schools, transport and fuel into nationalised organisations. Reorganisation, as in the NHS, cannot now come more often than, say, at 15-year intervals. Regional and local government has enlarged its activities, and made them more inflexible and "brittle." Government supplies more or less monopolised services. And, far from their mystical role as "public" services making the attitude of their trade unions more sensitive to the wants of the public, their economic power to pass on high wage costs in high consumer prices has made them more vulnerable to the pressures of trade unions.

It is thus hardly surprising that, not least in the two personally most sensitive state services, education and medical care, adaptation and reform are thwarted by the trade unions, or at least by the officialdom that claims to speak for the rank and file. Even local experiments in reform, such as the education voucher in Kent, or small-scale variations, such as the 1 per cent of beds for which patients sacrifice other comforts to pay for privacy or informal contact with family, are opposed or openly defied by the trade unions, or by officials who regard the "public" services as private preserves.

Yet it is misleading to blame the unions, and certainly misguided to condemn working people. Most union activities, even if sometimes bereft of brotherly idealism, rest on two sources of power, both created by government: the trade union law as passed by Conservative, Labour and Liberal governments in 1875, 1906, 1946 and 1975, and the market power created by nationalisation in fuel and transport, by the welfare state in education and medical care, and by the more recent expansion of local government services.

The Unions, the Law and State-Created Monopoly

It is not so much trade union members that should be blamed, nor even the officials that lead them, even though often elected by derisory minorities. To adapt Shakespeare: as long as the law allows it, and the artificial state monopoly awards it, the trade unions will not surprisingly exert their power. Nor is there refuge in the amiable tendency to personify the power politics of trade union bargaining: to suppose that, if only (say) Mr. David Basnett or Mr. Moss Evans or Mr. Clive Jenkins could be made to "see sense," all would be well. If "seeing sense" means settling for a lower wage than the state monopoly makes possible and the law allows the unions to enforce by strike-threat, picketing, immunity from action for damages, etc., the authority of the officials would be undermined by shop-stewards or others prepared to promise a harder line—as when incomes policies have widened the gap between approved and competitive pay. History and analysis indicate that the effective way to help Messrs. Basnett *et al* to "see sense," and retain the adherence of their members, is to repeal the privilege clauses of the 1906, 1946 and other Acts and to denationalise the state monopolies.

"Confrontation" or Appeasement

The risk as seen by some in the press, Parliament and industry, is "confrontation" with the unions. Is "confrontation" inevitable? Or is there a choice of "confrontations"?

The delicate question is whether continuing appeasement of a growing power outside Parliament, yet created or tolerated by government and the law, is permissible if it prevents the adaptation of the British economy to underlying changes in the conditions of supply and demand, a consequence especially debilitating for a country that has to export a fifth of her domestic product to maintain her living standards and her influence in the world.

Business men, politicians and journalists anxious to maintain social peace look to incomes policy as a means of avoiding "confrontation." Scarcity of resources impels man to make the best use of them. In so doing he must make difficult choices: in allocating resources of men, capital, land or money to some uses he must deny them to others. In a free society based on a market economy the "confrontations" take place on a small scale between buyers and sellers. And the differences are resolved by compromising on price. The larger the units of buyers and sellers, the larger the "confrontation," and the larger the risks to civil peace. And at the other extreme to the market, in the state economy, the "confrontations" are massive, since they are the outcome of power exercised by a handful of men over masses of other men.

There are thus two aspects of confrontation that should be clear. The first, and more immediate, is that appeasement brings only a short "peace." The choice is between little confrontations that ruffle tempers and big confrontations that risk social strife. The longer the "confrontation" is shirked, the more the paper tiger is pumped up into a bullfrog. The power of the trade unions does not lie so much in the power-hunger of trade union officials as in the failure to change the trade union law or to denationalise state monopolies—despite public opinion that would support both policies.

The second aspect is even more fundamental. The open society cannot long survive a power created or tolerated by Parliament that is invited to bargain with government. Down the centuries the British have disciplined the regional barons, the divine right of kings (bloodlessly in 1688 before it was too late, as the French found in 1789), the political church, the landowners, the House of Lords, monopoly business. The longer the disarmament of the monopoly unions is shirked, the more painful it will have to be. Even now it may be too late to disarm it without friction, as in the combative flying pickets of 1972 and the violent picketing at Grunwick of 1977. The unions, perhaps unjustly, are being seen for the first time among ordinary people, not least "working-class" wives, as engines of tyranny. Their tyrannical power to destroy the open society by repressing open debate is frighteningly illustrated in the reluctance of seven publishers to accept a book because, the author thought about several of them, it might upset the printers.[1] (Two said as much.) If the unions can prevent the publication of opinions they (or a handful of officials) dislike, Orwell's *1984* may not be long delayed. To suppress this consequence of continued appeasement is not to avoid confrontation but, by encouraging or misleading the unions, to provoke it.

Two important corollaries follow. First, those who wish to change society by revolution will resist small confrontations in the hope of building up steam for a disruptive "confrontation." Second, those who say "no confrontation" either knowingly promote or unknowingly acquiesce in the increasingly state-dominated post-war economy that creates tensions, discords, frictions, and larger confrontations by its incursion into private lives.

"Public" Goods and Social Conflict

Why has the scope for conflict been widened by government action and, less obviously but no less harmfully, inaction? Such are the issues—the role and function of government in causing *avoidable* social friction—that have been, not surprisingly, ignored by politicians and, more surprisingly, by social and political scientists. The unnecessary encroachment of the state into the provision of non-public goods, which it must decide by the only process it can use—the majority procedures of "representative" machinery—has created tensions by the resentment of more and more individuals that their lives are *unnecessarily* subjected to irrelevant and prejudiced political and politicised procedures.

It has long been argued by sociologists, typified by the late Richard Titmuss, and by some economists that social cohesion required the provision by government of common goods and services—education, medical care and others—to be jointly shared and used by individuals who would thus feel more securely bound to one another as members of a society. Conversely, individual activities that diverged or deviated from the common behaviour, not least private education and medical care, were regarded as creating "social divisiveness" and were therefore objectionable. This was, at

1. Sir John Colville, "Dryden and the Guilty Men," *Sunday Times*, 6 August 1978.

root, the moralistic/sociological rationale for (comprehensive) state education and the National Health Service, to which access was to be equal and unrestrained, and for the Welfare State in general. It is an ethos that still pervades all political parties. The more convincing explanation of social "divisiveness" is virtually the opposite: that, except in "public goods," the supply by government of monopoly or near-monopoly services from which there is no escape by people they do not satisfy destroys social cohesion and creates social divisiveness.

The claim of the state to provide the citizenry with indispensable goods and services is strongest in "public" goods. In a sentence, the term describes defence, law and order, public health protection against contagious disease and other such goods that must be provided by government (or other collective associations) and paid for by compulsory taxes "voluntarily" agreed (or rather decided by majority or other fraction less than 100 per cent) because they cannot be refused to people who refuse to pay.[2] These services must be supplied (or organised) by government or not at all. Government is not efficient at supplying them, since it cannot know individual preferences. It is almost certainly true that it does violence to individual wishes: thus the state may decide on 6 per cent of GNP as the optimum proportion to spend on defence, but individual preferences may vary from the pacifists' or Russophiles' 0 per cent to the Russophobes' 10 per cent. And much the same may be true of all other public goods. (A first attempt to measure the spread is made by the IEA in a new field survey in 1978.) But at least government has the reason of necessity for supplying public goods, and there is a general public sense that no other method is as feasible or convenient.

The issues are very different with non-public goods which do not have to be supplied by government at all. The arbitrariness, inequities, crudities and very rough justice in the decisions on the nature, scale and disposition of public goods are magnified many times in the use of the same political or committee majority machinery for non-public goods or services. Here is the genesis of potential social conflict in British society and elsewhere. Why?

Most of the activities of British government, national and local, are of this kind. It produces goods (coal, water, etc.) and services (transport, education, medical care, housing, libraries, fire services, job centres, refuse collec-

2. Technical accounts of "public goods" are in Maurice Peston, *Public Goods and the Public Sector,* Macmillan, 1972, and C. K. Rowley and A. T. Peacock, *Welfare Economics,* Martin Robertson, 1974. A simple short discussion is in A. Seldon, *Charge,* Maurice Temple Smith, 1977.

tion, even some police services, and many others) that it does not have to supply. And it does so by the same necessarily coercive machinery of committees of one kind or another ruled by majorities as for "public" goods. Moreover, the people sense it. That is the source of much of the incipient social tension, friction and conflict, which will intensify the more such services government supplies and the longer it supplies them.

There are various forms of social conflict generated by the sense that services are imposed on individuals by the unnecessary political coercion of other individuals who happen to have, or have had, the control of the machinery of government by temporary majority (or even *minority*). The forms of politically-created conflict are numerous; among them are:

1. *Regional/national:* the Scots may think the more numerous English and Welsh in Westminster decide their education, medical care, many other services (and the taxes to pay for them); so may the Welsh about the English and Scots.
2. *Sectarian/religious:* the Northern Irish Catholics are subjected to unnecessary coercion by the majority of Protestants who use the political process to decide their education, housing and other aspects of their private lives.
3. *Racial/religious:* coloured immigrants (and white minorities) are needlessly coerced into having their children educated in state schools designed by white, Protestant majorities. Pakistanis may wish their daughters to be taught in single-sex schools, Catholics in Catholic schools. All must pay taxes for schools decided by "representative" machinery in which they are out-voted.
4. *Fiscal/entrepreneurial:* the minority of risk-takers, innovators, the exceptionally talented (in art, culture, sport, etc.) and the highly skilled are coerced by the progressive taxation voted by the majority of security-seekers, non-innovators, modestly talented, medium- or low-skilled.
5. *Employment-status:* the minority of independent-spirited self-employed are coerced by legislation (on employment security, etc.) prejudicial to small-scale traders, professional advisers, etc. (and their employees) passed to appease the majorities employed by large-scale units.
6. *Occupational:* majorities of established doctors, actuaries, lawyers, architects, printers, engineers, dockers, etc., legally coerce minorities

of new entrants by acting as judge and jury in prescribing unnecessarily costly training, apprenticeship, superfluous staffing, demarcation or other protective devices.

7. *Familial:* minorities of parents, children and other relatives are legally coerced by political majorities into paying for medical care, education and other services they do not want, and are then virtually compelled by financial pressure to use them.
8. *Urbs in rure:* the activities of minority countrymen (fox-hunting, etc.) are inhibited or prohibited by laws enacted by "representatives" of town-dweller electoral majorities.
9. *Bureaucratic:* the minority of 4 million government employees, from teachers to messengers, exercise their influence over transient, amateur, pliant politicians to coerce the majority of private employees into paying for the unnecessary security of tenure, over-manning, inflation-proofed pensions, concealed leisure in working time, "eating for the Queen,"[3] excessive holidays of "public" (government) employees, and to pay for protected employment in relatively inefficient, high-cost, nationalised fuel, transport, education, medical care, or municipalised airports, libraries, refuse-collection, slaughterhouses, etc.
10. *Committee-government:* minorities of adroit, articulate activists use the committee machinery that controls state services (schools, hospitals, medical services, local authority services) to coerce majorities of maladroit, inarticulate inactivists.
11. *Sexual:* majorities of politically-minded men make national laws and local bye-laws that coerce majorities of domestically-inclined women.
12. *Elitist* (*reverse discrimination*)*:* minorities of would-be do-gooder élitists coerce the majority of pre-occupied citizens by preferment of minority-group individuals (poor, immigrant, coloured, etc.) over better-qualified majority-group individuals.[4]
13. *Cultural:* minorities of cultural élitists claiming "social benefits" use taxes to coerce the "uncultured" majority into financing minority arts: working-class soccer-goers subsidise middle-class opera-goers.

3. Professor Alan Peacock, in *The Economics of Politics,* Readings 18, IEA, 1978.

4. A young London woman, who found immigrants lower down the list preferentially rehoused, asked "Does my British birthright count for nothing?"

14. *Patrician:* the majority of viewers and listeners is unnecessarily coerced, and denied technically possible choice, by a tiny minority of "the great and the good," from Beveridge to Annan, that have advised continuing the artificial government control of broadcasting channels.
15. *Monopolistic:* trade unions are empowered by law to coerce the minority who would have obtained employment at lower pay by forcing (by threat of strike, etc.) higher pay for the majority of existing members.

Representative or Unrepresentative Government?

Students of "representative" democracy may observe that the advance of government beyond the realm of public goods and their invasion of the private domain makes democracy *unrepresentative.* In public goods, where economists are working on refinements of voting rules and electoral procedures,[5] voting machinery normally rests on majorities of one kind or another and coercion of minorities is unavoidable. (Quixotic voting systems may enable minorities to coerce majorities, as in the UK since 1945.) But in the provision of private benefits it is impossible to accept that the principle of "one-man-one-vote" applies to the machinery of elections, committees, boards of (school) governors, area health councils, and other nominally "representative" bodies that are supposed to reflect the opinion of total constituencies or populations. This machinery gives *more* than one vote to people who can organise and lobby and manage the machine, and *less* than one vote to individuals who lack these faculties, devices, skills and crafts. The advocate of massive or extended state control of services providing private benefits characteristically defends his case by claiming that the machinery is "representative" of, and accountable to, those who are intended to be benefited. In practice the claim cannot be substantiated. This is one more egalitarian myth.

Reaction from Coerced Individuals/Families

Most of these tensions and potential conflicts derive from stubborn use of political machinery to provide non-public goods that could be supplied to

5. Professor Gordon Tullock, a Founding Father of the economics of politics, discusses electoral machinery and other elements in "the theory of public choice" in *The Vote Motive,*

individual taste or family requirements in the market, and thus with little or no coercion of minorities. The tension will intensify in the coming five, ten or twenty years as public understanding of the *unnecessary* coercion to which individuals have been subjected in their intimate personal and family lives goes beyond resentment to rejection. For a century or more the British (and other peoples) have been induced by politicians into believing that government must supply not only the ("public") goods and services that only it can supply, and in which they therefore had to accept group majority or national decisions, but also a long and lengthening list of goods and services that the politicians insisted voters were not competent to decide for themselves as individuals or families (or smallish local, voluntary, "co-operative" groups). Their growing awareness of this political confidence-trick will be intensified by the reinforcement of their *anxiety* to exert individual preferences (to send a child to a school or hospital of the parents' choice, the most common examples so far), by the growing *ability* to exert the choice made possible by growing incomes (or by drawing on saving, or by mothers working). And the more their aspirations are thwarted by political insensitivity, bureaucratic obstruction or trade union resistance, the stronger the resentment will grow and the more strenuous the reaction will be. "Confrontation" is intensified by coercive representative majorities that invade private lives.

The six forms of reaction by coerced citizens have been analysed by Professor Charles Rowley[6] as "instruments of political participation": voting (for example, by "senior citizens"), pressure groups (junior doctors), social movements (leading, if unsatisfied, to civil disobedience by dispossessed professional groups), individual economic adjustment (tax avoidance leading to evasion,[7] leisure, malingering, do-it-yourself activities), revolution (or more likely *coups d'état* by small groups which avoid giving "free rides" to non-rebels), and emigration ("voting with one's feet") analysed in the relatively new economic theory of clubs.[8] There are examples in this book of all six reactions.

Hobart Paperback 9, IEA, 1976. More advanced discussion of "social welfare functions" is indicated by Professor Duncan Black in "On Arrow's Impossibility Theorem," *The Journal of Law and Economics,* The University of Chicago, 1969.

6. *The State of Taxation,* Readings 16, IEA, 1977, pp. 69–72.

7. Discussed in *Tax Avoision,* a forthcoming IEA Readings.

8. Charles Rowley, "Taxing in an International Labour Market," in *The State of Taxation, op. cit.,* pp. 73–4.

Recognition by Political Parties

There are indications that the possibility of growing reaction will be recognised in time. In all three political parties there is awakening anxiety about the subjection of the individual by the state. The contributions in this book from the three public men indicate anxieties that must be shared by others in their parties and could grow in time to obviate stronger reaction from individual citizens. Such development would not be surprising in the Conservative and Liberal Parties, although both have legacies of paternalism, benign or authoritarian. A Labour reaction against the state and in favour of the individual may be more surprising, but could be all the more significant. A new organisation, Mutual Aid Centre, formed by Lord (Michael) Young, a veteran Labour Party adviser, and Dr. Eric Midwinter of the National Consumer Council, is important both for its scepticism about the beneficence of the state and for its proposals of voluntary, co-operative activities. It creates a new approach sharply contrasted with the *étatism* that Labour has espoused since it was created in 1900.

A significant symptom of an emerging common approach among people in all three Parties is the interest in the education voucher, which is itself a tocsin that distinguishes those who approach policy-making through the state and through the individual. The Conservatives have taken the initiative in encouraging Kent County Council to initiate experimentation, Liberals have discussed a pressure group to promote the idea, and Labour intellectuals have been working on a "left-wing" version of a voucher. How far the impetus to create more effective parent-power has come from thinker-politicians and how far from dissatisfaction among parents will be for historians to judge. What seems clear is that Labour will have to decide, perhaps in the coming ten years, before 1989, whether it sides with "the workers" in education (and medical care and elsewhere), as represented or misrepresented by trade union officials, or with its historic constituency of working-class parents (and patients) growing out of their proletarian origins and increasingly able to pay school fees, health insurance premiums and mortgage instalments. "The workers" are "trading up," and the politicians will not suppress them.

Among Labour protestors at the inquisition or persecution by tax-gatherers of small-scale traders is a much respected Labour elder statesman, and an authority on the tax system. The necessary consequence of high taxation is the increasing powers of tax-inspectors to pursue taxpayers by new powers of entry (if necessary, by breaking into homes or offices), described by Lord (Douglas) Houghton as "the thin end of the wedge."[9]

> There is no justification for the prevailing philosophy among income tax men that they are entitled to parity of powers of forcible entry with the excise men. . . . if evasion is increasing, as it probably is, may the cause be that direct taxation in conditions of inflation and falling real standards have something to do with it?
>
> . . . [I]f so, the new power to . . . demand documents and the right to break-in . . . is not part of the battle against evasion so much as part of the counter-attack upon the resentful mood of the people. And I mean the people.
>
> The taxmen . . . are not noted for their interest in any civil liberties except their own. . . . [T]hey are not the best judges of the politics of taxation.

The flavour of these remarks re-appeared in an address by Lord Houghton to an IEA Seminar in 1977.[10]

Forms of Protest

A further consequential danger should be emphasised. Professor Rowley's "social movements" have appeared for some years in demonstrations, marches, sit-ins, and other forms of dramatised protest by parents (at William Tyndale School) and by people with more arguable causes—council tenants, hospital workers, students, and others. Democratic representative politicians and governments heed such activities both because they are ostensibly representative (at least of the articulate and the activist) and because they are noisy. Yet there is no more justice in yielding to noisy protests than to un-noisy resentment. The deeper-lying danger is that it teaches the normally quiet citizen that only noise wins attention. The argument was once put to a Labour Home Secretary: "If you yield only to those who march, you will induce ordinary people to take to the streets." That is what comes of destroying markets in which the individual citizen can "protest" by withdrawing his purchasing power and, without distressing confrontations,

9. *The Times,* 16 August 1976.
10. *The State of Taxation, op. cit.,* pp. 51–63.

moving quietly to a preferred supplier. Or will historians in the 1990s record accelerating skirmishes for good and bad causes? If they do, the blame will lie with those who prevented change by degree in the market.

The Market, "Planned Economy" and Direction of Labour

The logic of this analysis will be unpalatable to those who, possibly for the best of reasons, have looked to the state as the guarantor of distributive justice and democratic liberties. Lady (Barbara) Wootton persists in her belief over 40 years that only the state in "democratic socialism" can yield these fruits. I have long owed her a debt of gratitude since, as an undergraduate at the London School of Economics in the 1930s, I first learned from her *Plan or No Plan*[11] the massive superiority of the market ("no plan") over central direction of the economy ("plan"), even though her book was intended to teach the opposite. Forty years later she sticks to her guns in the best response she can muster[12] to the challenge to show where in the world civil liberties are respected in a socialist economy. The challenge, she affirms, is "easily met": what has not yet happened (that a socialist state so far *has* respected civil liberties) may yet happen (because rapid technical and social change will make them possible, or more likely). But neither has she demonstrated the opposite: that what *has* happened (no market: no civil liberty) will not recur. The onus of evidence is on her. For she is asking us to abandon the market, which *has* yielded personal liberties, for a non-market economy which, she agrees, has not "as yet permitted the political and civil freedoms now enjoyed by the British." The opponents of the market have thus abandoned confident assertion of the superiority of the state for defensive claims that, as a matter of faith, "checks and balances" will preserve basic liberties, although how or why is not explained.

Lady Wootton concedes that centralised planning may require direction of labour. Even more interesting is her new conclusion that, after all, markets have a useful role to play—as taught in the Yugoslav "self-regulating" enterprises or workers' co-operatives and the Hungarian shift from administrative order (central planning) to control by incentives (market devices).

Lady Wootton as economist at last sees the essence of the market—that it *dispenses* with autocratic or paternalistic central planning (and its built-in

11. Gollancz, 1934.

12. "Can We Still Be Democratic Socialists?: Why We Need a Planned Economy," *New Statesman*, 4 August 1978.

tensions and antagonisms). That new insight is still hidden from central planners who are not economists. Yet she and they still hanker after a dream-world of good men (and in these days we must add women) who will know enough of the people's individual preferences to be able to direct resources to serve them faithfully and efficiently. Economists until recently allowed political scientists such a lot of rope in pursuing the will-o'-the-wisp of men transformed into benefactors on election to "public" power or selection for "public" office that they have almost hanged themselves intellectually. The economists may yet save them by extending economics from the study of industry in the market with all its much-mulled-over imperfections to the study of politics (without markets) and all its long-neglected imperfections.[13] I suspect political scientists will be learning more from economists in the next few years about the working of political government than economists have learnt from political scientists about the working of the market.

Conserving Institutions or Principles

A parallel dilemma faces those at the other extreme of the philosophic spectrum who so fear the uncertainties of reform that, like Sir Ian Gilmour,[14] Mr. William Waldegrave[15] and Mr. Maurice Cowling,[16] they look to continuity, tradition and custom to safeguard the civilised values of society. This approach would preserve established institutions but risk loss of the purposes and principles they were erected to serve. They would preserve practices of which they do not approve, like trade union and professional closed shops and other legal immunities and privileges, because sanctified by usage. But they make the same mistake as the opponents of "confrontation": by opposing small-scale reform in the market they do not avoid change but make it more discontinuous, and thus risk the very continuity they hope to preserve.

Long-Term Economic Consequences of Political Acts

Such are the long-term consequences of short-term policies that the essays in this book are intended to explore. They indicate that much or most

13. *The Economics of Politics, op. cit.*
14. *Inside Right,* Hutchinson, 1977.
15. *The Binding of Leviathan: Conservatism and the Future,* Hamish Hamilton, 1978.
16. *Conservative Essays,* Cassell, 1978.

of the thinking in the last 30 years—and further back for about a century—will have to be abandoned. It offered *short*-term solutions to immediate problems—poverty, unemployment, inflation, inequality in education, medical care and housing, sluggish rates of economic growth—but at a cost in *long*-term effects for which no politician or government will accept the blame but which our children, our grandchildren and our country will suffer: unemployment, inflation, failure to keep pace not only with our neighbours and the rest of the world but, even worse, with our own past, so that Britain must be denied the improvements that could come from the advance of science and influence in world affairs.

Reasons for Hope

Yet there are five reasons for hope. The most immediate and elemental is the growing resistance of the family to invasion by the state. The family is the protector of private lives that the state invades at its peril. Resistance will come in the two most intensely personal services wrongly provided by the state: medical care and education. When parents are prevented from spending their money on a kidney machine to save their child's life and fathers are prepared to be imprisoned rather than see their children sent to schools decided by officials to suit the system, it cannot be long before politicians see that state medicine and schooling will require intensifying coercion that the British people will increasingly resist. Tax-evasion will be accompanied by state-evasion. Unless the state introduces tax credits or vouchers, by which all who feel oppressed can escape, only the better off or self-sacrificing who pay (taxes) for services they do not use as well as (prices) for services they prefer will be able to escape. And, as incomes rise, there will be no way to stop the increasing number from escaping, short of destroying the open society. Instead of creating equality of access, the state therefore will have created inequality of exit. The egalitarians are surprisingly slow to see this development. Yet it is possible to envisage a growing demand by families for private medical care and education better than the state can provide equally for all out of taxation. The market could satisfy that demand; only the state could suppress it. Yet the egalitarians again do not see the potential social conflict in the "confrontation" of new private aspirations and state standardisation.

Second, the resistance of the family will be reinforced by the approaching equality and the emerging influence of woman. As wife, mother and daughter (and to a lesser degree as a less close relative) she will prefer markets to governments. She does the household as well as the personal buying, she shops around, she compares prices, she knows the power over the shopkeeper of the ability to shop elsewhere by taking her purchasing power with her. In her wish to do the best for her family she is more concerned than man with take-home pay that she spends than with the social wage that others spend for her. She is less exposed than man to accept mass decisions, or moral pressure, in factory, trade union, or political meetings. She feels herself less a member of a group or a class than an individual. She has less concern about social cohesion than about family well-being. She is less moved by abstract notions than by everyday realities. In short, she is unconsciously more than man in favour of the market and more frustrated than man by the coercive majority machinery of public choice that prevents her from doing what she does best. Rising incomes will reinforce her micro-attitudes. By now micro-woman would have laughed out of court, and destroyed by derision, the schoolboy pretensions of macro-man to run complex industrialised society by a coterie of élitists. That may be why the matriarchal society of America is based on the market and the patriarchal society of Russia tries to run itself from the centre. And that is why emerging micro-woman in Britain will increasingly assert the family against the state.[17]

It is probably, moreover, the "working-class" wife, armed with new purchasing power to buy "middle-class" comforts, not least when her children want them most, who will reject the burgeoning welfare state and its high taxation that reduces her husband's take-home pay. It is from the lower but rising income groups, therefore, that the rejection of the state in favour of the market is the more likely. The visitor to market-orientated Japan, Taiwan and Hong Kong can have little doubt where the preferences of emerging peoples will lie. In the nineteenth century the market replaced state regulation despite what John Stuart Mill called "The Subjection of Women." In the twentieth century the market could be all the more strengthened by the assertion of woman.

Third, government will find it more difficult to raise revenue because of the growing anxiety about the corrupting effects of high and rising taxes. The "tax revolt" in Britain began long before the Referendum on Proposition 13 in California. The revolt has been accelerating; and politicians in all parties are recognising it. Mr. Callaghan has said "[people] want less tax and

17. Fortunately micro-woman is more numerous than macro-woman who, like macro-man, claims to know how other people should live and would compel them by majority rules.

more money in their pockets." There is little reason to suppose they will "want" higher taxes at any time in the future.

They are resisting it by what might be called tax "avoision," an unconscious rejection of the moral difference between legal avoidance and illegal evasion, that is spreading in all social classes. The difficulty of raising revenue may induce government to reserve for public goods the revenue it can raise, and to finance by varying forms of charging the wide array of separable private benefits it has been adding to its functions. Charging would not only raise revenue but also lead to a more rational allocation of functions by channelling private services to the market. If people have to pay out of pocket for state benefits formerly free or subsidised, they will prefer to pay for private service with more choice and authority over the supplier. The state sector will therefore be reduced to comprise essentially public goods.

Fourth, it cannot be much longer before intellectuals of all schools, not least with Labour sympathies, see that there was never a case for universal, all-embracing, exclusive, state medicine or schooling (or any private services). The most the advocates of the (supposed) benefits of state control could claim was a trial for a period in one region (or more) to demonstrate whether or not the hoped-for good results were likely to be reproduced on a national scale. But without a jot of evidence they introduced exclusive systems, and moreover resist criticism, comparison and reform. After 30 years of the NHS they assume or claim another 30 years to remove its defects.[18]

Even then there is a further hurdle to surmount. If the condition for the effectiveness of state medicine or education is the exclusion of all other systems to prevent creaming off, say, doctors or high-ability children, the lost opportunity of discovering better systems is too high a price to pay. I do not see how any political or social scientist can believe the contrary. This is at bottom the flaw of all exclusive systems, whatever compassionate labels they give themselves.

Moreover, there has never been a popular vote in favour of a *permanent* National Health Service or comprehensive state schooling. Until there are single-policy referenda (with price-tags for alternatives), no British government can claim a mandate for any of its policies, except on public goods. Public understanding of this confidence trick also is awakening.

Fifth, again except in public goods, the market finds its way back, or

18. An example in an otherwise acute observer is Professor Rudolf Klein: "Who Decides? Patterns of Authority," *British Medical Journal*, 1 July 1978; and "An Unquestionable British Success," *The Times Higher Education Supplement*, 21 July 1978.

rather people find their way to it. Sixty years ago in a minor classic the Austrian economist Böhm-Bawerk[19] argued that political power would sooner or later succumb to economic law, the market. That is, politicians would have to defer to the people, who are uniquely enfranchised by it. Countries that have tried to suppress the market have had to restore it sooner or later, or suffer confusion or chaos. When they restore it, the rulers' power is shifted to "market forces," in other words, ordinary men and women; so they suppress it, until chaos returns. These countries have demonstrated by such alternations that in practice the alternative to the market is coercion. And that is why the British, who have seen the market increasingly suppressed or repressed, and can now judge the results, will want to restore it—not least in medicine and education, where it was said to be least practicable.

All this because we thought we could avoid the discomforts of change by obstructing change itself. If this is what people are thought to want, let them be told the price. And let *them* make the choice. Until that choice is explained and exercised, the suspicion must be that those who stand by the state fear that the verdict of the people will be peaceful change through the market. The "confrontation" with truth, so long delayed by unproved and untested hypotheses spuriously invested with political authority, by the élitist preference for "public" over private, and by unfounded fear of inevitable and beneficial change, may come before or after 1989. The sooner the better for the prospect of preserving and strengthening the open society that Britain gave the world by precept and example.

19. "Political Power or Economic Law?" 1914; reprinted in the *Shorter Classics of Böhm-Bawerk*, Libertarian Press (South Holland, Ill., USA), 1962.

INDIVIDUAL LIBERTY, PUBLIC GOODS, AND REPRESENTATIVE DEMOCRACY

Individual Liberty, Public Goods, and Representative Democracy

Lessons from the West and Escape for the East

> If it is assumed that whatever the majority decides is just, even if what it lays down is not a general rule, but aims at affecting particular people, it would be expecting too much to believe that a sense of justice will restrain the caprice of the majority: in any group it is soon believed that what is desired by the group is just.
>
> . . . since the theoreticians of democracy have for over a hundred years taught the majorities that whatever they desire is just, we must not be surprised if the majorities no longer even ask whether what they decide is just. Legal positivism has powerfully contributed to this development by its contention that law is not dependent on justice but determines what is just.
>
> F. A. Hayek, *Economic Freedom and Representative Government,* Institute of Economic Affairs, London, 1973.

> If . . . dividing supreme power into two independent democratic assemblies, or some better device, is not applied in the next 10 years or so, the public loss of faith in the ideal of democracy itself will continue to evaporate, especially if government acquires even more power over economic life and even more power to dispense arbitrary, discriminate benefits to group interests that will, in turn, therefore, be increasingly disposed to organise pressure on it.
>
> F. A. Hayek, *The Coming Confrontation,* Institute of Economic Affairs, London, 1978.

As incomes rise in Western societies, individuals can pay more for more goods and services in the market, yet government has paradoxically taken more of them in taxes and supplied more goods and services in return. As incomes become more equal by the operation of competition, contract and mobility, the "free" supply by government of goods and services financed by redistributive, "progressive" taxation becomes less necessary, desirable or justifiable; yet taxes become increasingly generalised payment for government supply. This twin quixotic development requires more attention from market economists concerned with the translation of economic liberalism into public policy.

I. Growth of Government: West and East

Relatively to the rising trend in real income, the individual in Europe, North America and Australasia (although probably not in the market oases of Taiwan, South Korea or Hong Kong and elsewhere in Asia) has been losing control over the disposition of his income. An expansion in public goods, not least defence to protect societies against Communist expansion, might explain and justify a larger proportion of even rising real income being taken in taxes. But most of the increasing taxes have been taken to provide wholly or largely private goods and personal benefits that could have been supplied by developing markets.

Even in the market oases of Asia, not least Taiwan and Hong Kong, the same false justification for higher "public" (government) expenditure is heard from government officials and other advisers urging politicians to take the fiscally easy and (wrongly thought) politically popular course of raising more revenue from rising incomes to provide more private goods, not least education and medical care, on the ground that, as economic growth makes these societies richer, they can "afford" to spend more on public benefits. Politicians in emerging societies would be better advised to observe where this schoolboy howler of a *non sequitur* and circular reasoning has led the liberal West.

It may already have occurred to the more astute of public men in the East as well as the West that rising real incomes may make it *possible* for government to raise more tax revenue to spend on "free" (or nominally-priced) government services but also make it *unnecessary,* since by definition rising personal real incomes enable more people to pay more in the market. In the market oases less government expenditure on public health and associated environmental services has been made possible by the conquest of infectious and contagious disease. The argument for more expenditure on measures to contend with the pollution externalities of noise, smell and congestion is over-exaggerated because it does not always allow for the extent to which the externalities can be internalised by pricing. And the new public health service of information to inculcate living habits that preserve health, now gaining credence in the West, is likely to require far less revenue than the nineteenth century public health measures against infection and contagion.

The East, moreover, could learn from the West, especially Britain, about the political difficulty of phasing out private/personal benefits as incomes rise, even where the reasons for installing them had been valid in the first place.

II. False Arguments for Government Supply of Private Goods

In Britain, and in much of Western Europe, the justifications for the government supply of the largely non-public goods, especially education and medical care, the two largest state benefits in kind that with other social benefits comprise a half of British government (central and local) expenditure, go back a century, from poverty in the 1860s to Keynesian demand management since the 1940s.

The medley of arguments, justifications and pretexts numbers mainly nine, and they have not been adequately contested. The nineteenth century argument of ("primary") poverty was that many people lacked the earnings or wealth to pay for the desirable quantum of education, medical care and other "social services." The later argument of irresponsibility, dignified by Seebohm Rowntree and other British observers of social conditions as "secondary poverty," was that, even where earnings or wealth became adequate, they would not necessarily be used to pay for the desired services. After R. H. Tawney came the argument of equality developed by the Fabians and R. M. Titmuss: only state supply, they insisted, could ensure equality of access. A fourth argument, derived from the sociologists, was the parity of esteem that again required government supply rather than payment in the market. The fifth argument was Fabian-economic: centralised government supply of transport and power reaped the economies of large-scale technique, financing, and management. The sixth argument, of similar vintage, was that transport and power for lighting and heating was a "natural monopoly" requiring the power of eminent domain to facilitate lowest-cost production and distribution. The seventh, and more recent, was, and is, the argument of externality—that some services would be under-produced in the market because they rendered "social benefits" the value of which individuals would not comprehend and for which they would not voluntarily pay; they would therefore have to be taxed and so be forced to pay indirectly for collective production on the required larger scale. The opposite proposition, that some products/services, which imposed "social costs" on third parties who could not be compensated, would therefore be over-produced in the market, formed the eighth argument for government supply. (Since all goods/services have external effects, benefits or costs, if the legal framework is not designed to internalise all externalities, there was nothing left for the market at all.) The ninth argument was the most generalised: government had to control enough of total expenditure (whether, it seemed, there was any justification for individual items or not) to be able to offset fluctuations in private demand in the market, and so keep the economy on an even keel and avoid the opposite excesses of under-employment and over-exuberant price rises.

All of these nine justifications of government expenditure have been rejected, some in recent years. Keynesian countervailing "public" expenditure does not survive the combined critique of Friedman-ite monetarist diagnosis of inflation and unemployment and Buchanan-ite dissection of the *political* inability of government to offset budget surpluses symmetrically with deficits.[1] The appeal to social cost has been undermined by the explanation that divergences between private and social costs and benefits can often be removed by shifting the boundaries of property rights so that effects that were external can be made internal. "Natural monopoly" and economies of large scale that produce monopoly are better left in private hands even if subject to anti-trust law, because they do not survive innovation which introduces new techniques that reap more economies from medium or small scales; in contrast, state control confirms and perpetuates the monopoly, which then requires economic, political and social upheaval to dislodge. Equality and parity of esteem are even more remote in the state economy, where access is determined by differences in political, cultural, racial, religious, class, economic or other forms of power, in which the lowly (the "disadvantaged," "under-privileged" and "deprived" of the new sociology) cannot hope to achieve equality, than in the market, where the inequality of income and wealth can more readily be corrected. Irresponsibility is itself the result of the divorce between payment and service that is the hallmark of state supply of "free" services. And poverty does not require state supply but state redistribution of tax revenue to "top up" low incomes by purchasing power, untied in cash or earmarked by voucher.

1. J. M. Buchanan and R. E. Wagner, *Democracy in Deficit: The Political Legacy of Lord Keynes,* New York and London, 1977. The argument is refined and applied to the British economy in J. M. Buchanan, John Burton and R. E. Wagner, *The Consequences of Mr. Keynes,* Institute of Economic Affairs, London, 1978.

The case for state supply of services, except public goods, has for a century been the creation of intellectuals, a gigantic hoax on the common people that politicians from Bismarck, through Roosevelt to Bevan and Butler have gladly embraced because it validated their urge for power, which they variously rationalised as compassion, public service or patriotism. The growth of the state since the nineteenth century has been the tragedy of the West that will destroy civilisation if it is not resisted and itself destroyed. It has destroyed the individual spirit in Eastern Europe, in large parts of China, and is spreading to Africa where it will probably require armed revolution to overthrow. The market oases of Asia can resist it before it grows further. In the Western World it will now require tenacious strategies to resist and repulse.

III. Weakness in the Case for Government Supply

It is surprising that, despite the intellectual weakness of the arguments for enlarging the province of the state, and their rebuttal by a long line of liberal economists, political scientists, philosophers and historians from David Hume and Adam Smith 200 years ago to Karl Popper and Friedrich Hayek in our day, the expansion of the state has proceeded remorselessly. Two kinds of emergencies—war and slump—gave power-hungry politicians the plausible excuse that in crises there was no time for the niceties of intellectual argument about the relative merits of market and state in economic affairs. The growth of the state began a century ago in Britain, but was first accelerated to formidable proportions by the 1914–18 war and then by the 1930–33 depression. It was further enlarged during and after the 1939–45 war. It is difficult to believe that the British Welfare State would have been created in 1946–48 if it had not rested on false analogy with the community action of the war years, and if economists and others, many absorbed in supervising and then running down war-time controls, had been able to put the case against state welfare. Without the 1939–45 war it is doubtful if Keynesian deficit financing or the Beveridge-Bevan-Butler welfare state would have been established.

Even so, liberals could have deployed more effectively two arguments against the expansion of the state that might have weighed with what Hayek has called the "second-hand dealers in ideas" who shape opinion and influence policymakers, and even with power-hungry politicians.

First: however plausible any of the nine arguments for expanding the state, they remained hypotheses difficult to rebut conclusively since the unknown is always possible. The most their protagonists—Conservatives like Bismarck in Germany, "liberals" in the USA like Roosevelt, liberal economists in Britain like Beveridge, Socialist ideologues like Bevan, Conservative politicians like Butler—could claim was small-scale pilot experiments to discover whether the hypotheses were supported by testing in the real world of fallible men, imperfect institutions, self-interested bureaucracies. If they were not rebutted by successive experimentation they might then be extended on a larger scale.

Second: even if experimentation had suggested that state supply had advantages that justified wider application, which I doubt, there was never under any circumstances, even those of war or slump, a conclusive case for establishing it on a national scale with power to exclude other methods, techniques or systems. For to do so would be to exclude the possibility of discovering even better methods, techniques or systems that might emerge with the evolution of individual aspirations, social institutions, industrial or commercial innovation. But if no other method, technique or system could emerge because it was suppressed, the only way of demonstrating that state supply was the best system available to man would have been destroyed. However plausible the hypothesis in favour of state supply, and however persuasive the evidence of success in early experiments, the exclusion of alternatives was too high a price to pay for *exclusive* state supply.

There is therefore never, under any circumstances, and even, as Professor W. A. Niskanen[2] has demonstrated, in public goods such as armament research and manufacture, a conclusive case for abolishing the market. That is the truth that liberals in Europe, North America and Australasia have failed to press home with sufficient intellectual tenacity on opinion-formers and policy-makers against the infinitely inferior case for exclusive state supply. Fortunately it is not too late to do so in the Western world or in Asia.

There are reasons for supposing this truth will be heeded more in the future than in the past. For there is now evidence from the thirty years of British post-war experience that state supply has failed. How far the lessons will be learned and applied will depend on the resistance from the older ideas favouring state supply, from the institutions created by state supply, and from the interests that would lose income or property if state supply were run down—government employees organised in trade unions and profes-

2. *Bureaucracy and Representative Government,* Chicago, 1971; *Bureaucracy: Servant or Master,* Institute of Economic Affairs, London, 1973.

sional associations with bureaucratic power to influence the course and pace of events.

Two examples from Britain may suffice to illustrate these possibilities, tendencies to reform, and resistances to change. They also indicate the lessons that other Western countries and the emerging market societies of the East could learn if they are not too blind to see.

The case for the British *National* Health Service or for British *universal* comprehensive state education is intellectually so weak that no social political scientist should have given it a moment's credence. Yet, under the influence of political ideologues and bureaucratic trade unions, medical care and education in Britain are being made monopolies that are gradually excluding any alternative method, technique or system of organising medical care or education. The wholly state-owned hospitals in the National Health Service, for example, are gradually ejecting the one per cent of "pay" beds for which patients could pay for a choice of doctor, privacy, maintenance of contact with family or work, or personal comforts. Politicians are allowing nonmedical employees such as porters organised in trade unions to have more authority in decisions on medical treatment. And all state schools are gradually being standardised into "comprehensives" in which children of all rates of intellectual advance are taught together, and private schools in which children of similar intellectual capacity are taught together are discouraged. All this—and much more—is being done in the name of equality and the "right" of employees to have decisive influence on the conduct of the "public" services in which they work.

These developments are proceeding without evidence that the hypothesis—that "employee participation" will improve the National Health Service, or that quicker children will galvanise the slower to work and learn more quickly—are substantiated in practice. The sanctity of equality is used to reinforce these trends to exclusive monopoly state supply.

I must add that there are economists and other academics who support the trend not only to state supply but to state monopoly in both. Here is a development that liberals in the West and the East must recognise quickly before it is too late. As state supply extends, it is natural for the state to encourage and finance research into ways of improving the efficiency of its services in order, if nothing more, to win popular support for them and to reduce its requirement of tax revenue. It is also natural for the state to ignore or discourage research into ways of improving on state supply, which in practice means discovering ways of making the market work better.

Such developments would have appalled liberals in the nineteenth century. They should be used by liberals in our day to condemn the politicians, academics and others who tolerate them without thought for their consequences for the future of civilisation.

IV. The Political Creation of Social Conflict

The fundamental flaw in, and the fearsome consequences of, the growth of the state in Western society are clear. The error is that the state has used the same political machinery for private goods that it has to use for deciding the nature and scale of public goods.

The state decides the nature and scale of public goods by majority decisions and committee procedures. Majorities of citizens elect political parties into power, and they in turn decide by majorities in Parliaments or other legislatures or in Cabinet Rooms how much to raise in tax revenue and how to distribute it between defence and other public goods.

1. The Misuse of Political Machinery for Private Goods

This is the only method government can use. It is crude, arbitrary, clumsy and wasteful, since it does not reflect individual preferences. Refinements are possible: two-thirds or other proportions instead of simple majorities; proportional representation in varying forms to replace first-past-the-post majority voting and prevent government based on minorities; referenda or plebiscites on single issues, or small groups of issues, instead of crude take-it-or-leave-it votes for or against all 27, 49 or 163 planks in the platforms of political parties; varying devices from entrenched clauses to Supreme Courts to prevent governments elected by temporary majorities from riding roughshod over minorities; and others. But there is nothing better that government can do to respect and reflect individual preferences, or the preferences of small groups or uncommon minorities. Since public goods are defined as those that cannot be refused to people who refuse to pay for them, they must be financed by voluntary agreement to pay "compulsorily" by taxes. And tax revenues must be spent by the decisions of majorities and committees.

As government in Britain, and elsewhere in the West, has extended to embrace personal/private services, it has used essentially the same majority/committee procedures to decide the distribution of tax revenues between state education, health care, housing subsidies, pension subsidies (through so-called "social insurance") and many more. The most it can do to respect and reflect the preferences of small groups (but not individuals) is to decentralise such personal/private services to regional or local authorities. But even here decentralisation is limited by the collectivist/egalitarian anxiety to avoid differences between richer and poorer areas, which in Britain are reduced by "block grants" from central government, thus restoring the reality of central state control over education, medical care, housing, and many other nominally "local" services.

This is the flaw in the conduct of state-provided private/personal services. The consequence is a vast growth in *unnecessary* social conflict. There is increasing personal dissatisfaction with government services, especially the most intimate of education and medical care that affect the concern of husbands and wives for each other and of parents for infant and adolescent children: increasingly they feel their family lives are ruled by outsiders. And there is intensifying tension between minorities and majorities because of the electoral power of majorities to decide how minorities shall live. No wonder, as Hayek says, groups organise themselves to influence legislatures.

In Britain, as in the USA, there is increasing anxiety to escape from standardised "public services." If individuals were given the choice between paying taxes for government services and paying in the market for private/personal services more nearly "tailored" to their individual or family circumstances, requirements and preferences, many more than now would prefer to pay in the market. In Britain there is no such choice: an individual who would rather pay in the market for a private service has also to pay government for the "public" service he does not use. Short of such a choice in practice, a second-best method of discovering private preferences is the field survey of a national sample asked to state its preferences between the two alternatives, *with their relative costs indicated as nearly as possible.*

The two very different results are highly revealing. In the absence of a clear choice, roughly 5% of British families contract out of state education, despite paying taxes for it, and pay in the market for private education; and roughly 2½% contract out of the National Health Service (or most of it) despite paying taxes for the whole of it, and also pay in the market, through insurance, for private medical care. In contrast, with price-labels attached to both to make the preference significant since demand is meaningless without reference to price, the Institute of Economic Affairs has revealed that the true order of magnitude of the preference for private over government services has risen from 30% for education in 1965 to 52% in 1978, and from 30% for medical care to 58%.[3] The early results of these pioneering researches into these hypothetical demand curves, which indicate the reality behind the crude public choices made in the ballot box and the widespread inability to relate "public" service benefits to their costs in taxes, attracted the attention of Professor J. M. Buchanan who discussed them in his celebrated pioneering *Public Finance in Democratic Process* in 1965, subtitled "Fiscal Institutions and Individual Choice."

These findings indicate the massive suppression of individual preferences by a state system that does not allow contracting out. Little wonder that more and more British citizens feel they are locked into a state system from which they cannot escape except by the large penalty of "paying twice"—once in their taxes for the state service they want to reject and once in prices (fees, charges, insurance premiums, etc.) for the private service they prefer.

2. Rising Tide of Resentment and Social Conflict

This sense of resentment is producing more explicit tension and conflict as individuals come to understand that their denial of personal choice, their dissatisfactions, "imprisonment," and the political and bureaucratic lack of respect for their private personal or family sensitivities, are *unnecessary.* It is the consequence of using the majority/committee procedure of the political process in the ballot box for services in which, I would argue, the British increasingly sense that it is technically feasible for them to increase personal choice by rejecting the unsatisfying (state) supplier. Moreover they know that their rising incomes would enable them to pay (in the market) if they did not have to "pay twice." This growing social conflict arising from the resentment against the coercion of majorities takes numerous forms in Britain. (There are parallels in the USA, Europe, Australia, Asia and Africa.)

a. Regional (National)

A regional, or national, form is that of the people of Scotland and Wales who (rightly) resent the political majority power of the more numerous English to decide the education, medical care and many other personal services the people of Scotland and Wales must use, and pay for in taxes (unless they

3. The measure was calculated as the response to education and health vouchers worth ⅔ of the cost of paying for a private service. If the voucher had represented the full cost, the responses would presumably have been higher, and the increase faster: Ralph Harris and Arthur Seldon, *Over-ruled on Welfare*, IEA, London, 1979.

pay twice). A religious or sectarian form of social conflict arises from resentment of the Catholics of Northern Ireland that so-called "social" but essentially personal services (not least housing) are decided by majorities of Protestants. Within England (and Scotland and Wales and Northern Ireland) racial/religious tension is created among minorities of Catholics, Baptists, Jews and, more lately, Pakistanis who must send their children to schools decided by white, Anglo-Saxon, Protestant majorities. In all three cases there would be less coercion and less social tension, and therefore less cause for "nationalism" in Scotland, civil war (since 1969) in Northern Ireland, and disaffection in England, if the state withdrew from personal "social" services and confined itself to public goods. The Scots, the Catholics, the Jews and Pakistanis would still be outvoted on defence, etc., where opinion does not run on national or religious lines, but not on the conditions of their intimate personal and family lives.

b. Occupational

A second group of social tensions is occupational. The minority of risk-takers, innovators, exceptionally talented (in art, culture, sport, etc., as well as industry and commerce) and the exceptionally skilled are pillaged and coerced by the progressive taxation voted by the majority of people who seek security, are not innovators, are only modestly talented, or are unskilled or medium-skilled. The minority of self-employed who are entrepreneurially-minded and independent-spirited are coerced by legislation on employment security, etc., passed by government to appease the large majorities of employees. Established majorities of doctors, actuaries, lawyers, architects, printers, dockers and others are enabled by politically-created legal privileges to exclude minorities of would-be new entrants by prescribing unnecessarily costly training or apprenticeship, superfluous staffing (transport, printing, etc.), and other protective devices.

c. Bureaucratic/Syndicalist

A third form of friction is created by the use by minorities of articulate activists and manipulators of the political majority/representative/committee system, particularly in education and medical care, to dominate or coerce majorities of passive citizens, who moreover tend to be in the lower-income groups. The "representative" committee which has to operate in the absence of a pricing mechanism has lately been claimed in Britain by the supporters of state economy, notably Mr. Anthony Wedgwood Benn, the energetic Minister for Energy, to be more democratic than the market because it is "accountable" to the citizen who elects it and whom it "represents." This new apologia has been made necessary by the growing disillusionment with conventional "public ownership" (nationalisation) of fuel, transport, education and medical care, because of bureaucratic remoteness and insensitivity to individual circumstances, and the growing syndicalist tendency of the employees, reinforced by laws that endow their trade unions with privileges, to regard the "public services" primarily as means of maintaining jobs and only secondarily as services for the consumer.

d. Cultural, Sexual, Urban/Rural

Yet a fourth form of friction derives from the realisation that cultural elites derive privileges for themselves from government subsidies for minority arts (opera, museums, etc.) at the expense of the majority of (usually lower-paid) taxpayers who hardly use them.

A source of friction exploited by Women's Liberationists to demand "equal rights" even in unique circumstances (such as equal pensions despite differences in life expectancy) is the use of the legislature by majorities of politically active men to pass laws that coerce majorities of domestically-minded women.

A recent form of friction is a small but telling example of the tyrannical use by majority power in representative democracy. Politicians with strong support in large towns have moved to outlaw rural pursuits such as fox-hunting by relatively small minorities of countrymen.

Inequality in Income and Power. Critics of the market complain that people with relatively low income or wealth have less purchasing/voting power in the market than others with relatively high income or wealth. They therefore advocate one-man-one-vote in the polling booth (to by-pass inequality of income/wealth) as the more equitable democratic system of deciding the use of resources. This was the impetus behind the British Welfare State, the American Great Society, Swedish Social Democracy and other manifestations of state supply. And, until the last 10 years or so, liberal economists and politicians in Britain paid too little attention to means of evening up incomes without disproportionately adverse effects on incentives.

Yet, even without such measures as negative (or reverse) income taxes or vouchers, liberal economists could have pointed to what was evident from history down the centuries, and not least in Soviet Russia. They could have replied that, if there is no market in which each man's pound or dollar, or

Deutschmark, or franc is the same as everyone else's, access will be based on much more arbitrary differences in power, cultural or political, that are more difficult to correct or remove. None of the tensions and incipient conflicts reviewed above can be removed by re-arranging voting systems, making "representative" institutions more "accountable," or devising constitutional safeguards for minorities. Given the political machinery of majority decisions by representatives, the only way the Catholics of Northern Ireland can remove their vulnerability to dominance by Protestant majority is by shooting Protestants and breeding Catholics, so that the Protestant majority is replaced by a Catholic majority. But that would replace Protestant dominance by Catholic dominance, and Catholic grievance by Protestant grievance. And much the same is true of the other forms of friction. There is no solution by political/constitutional reforms so long as government provides private goods.

The only certain method of removing the friction is to remove its cause: the power of majorities to coerce minorities, or of minorities with power to coerce majorities without power. That means depriving men of power over the personal/private lives of other men, and confining political majority decisions to public goods. If the Catholics in Northern Ireland were not taxed to finance schools (or housing) controlled by Protestants but initially had vouchers, and ultimately kept their taxes, so that they could pay fees (or rents) for schools (housing) of their choice, there would be much less cause for avoidable friction. They might still dislike the choices of the Protestants in public goods, but they could no more complain that the Protestants did not make Catholic choices than claim they would make Protestant choices.

The market minimises *group* conflict; state economy maximises group conflict. Liberal economists have not exploited the strength of their case to the full.

V. Social Welfare Function and Individual Frustration

The state economy also maximises *individual* frustration; and the market minimises it.

The "social welfare function" was a figment of the state planners' imagination, or a product of the wishful thinking that individual preferences could be assimilated in broad categories sufficiently to make allocation by central authority of resources among competing employments feasible, and more equitable and efficient than in a market order. Although Arrow recognised the impossibility of such a theorem, the suspicion or hope that it might one day be found practicable lingers on. J. M. Buchanan has said[4] that, although Arrow conceded the impossibility, he "would have been happier if he could have been able to demonstrate that a social welfare function could be constructed," and he "was, and to my knowledge remains, an advocate of social planning." Collective choice theorists continue to examine the restrictions on individual preferences required to generate consistent social orderings.

Opponents of the market claim that government can or would reflect public preferences more faithfully. What evidence is there for or against this view? In theory it would be feasible to erect a structure of prices and purchasing power, and see how citizens expressed their preferences. I have described above how wide a gap there is in Britain between freely expressed preferences and government allocation of resources. In public goods, supplied collectively and consumed jointly by the populace, no private preferences can be elicited by such "second-best" methods. But more can be done by adapting techniques than has been done by government to validate its claims to serve the national interest by reflecting public preferences. The only evidence it can now point to is that the electorate elects one political party rather than another; and it claims that electoral approval provides evidence of agreement with the elected party's policies.

This is a very unconvincing assertion. First, even the claim to represent a majority cannot be supported; since the 1939–45 war every British government, Conservative or Labour, has been elected by a minority of votes cast (and by as little as a third or a quarter of the total electorate). Second, there has often been little or no choice between the two main parties.[5] Third, there has never so far been an opportunity to indicate preferences on single issues, as there are in Swiss referenda or American "propositions." The only issue put to the vote has been on constitutional matters: adherence to the Common Market (in June 1976) and Scottish/Welsh devolution (March 1979). Otherwise both parties have opposed referenda. Neither therefore can claim to have "represented" the electorate because it has never given them the opportunity to record a clear vote in support of any single one of its policies—from the National Health Service in 1946 to the trade union closed shop in 1974.

4. *The Economics of Politics*, Readings 18, Institute of Economic Affairs, London, 1978.

5. As Professor Gordon Tullock has led us to expect, their policies tended to converge: they were described jocularly or cynically as Butskellism (after the Conservative R. A. Butler and the Socialist Hugh Gaitskell) in the 1950s and MacWilsonism (after the Conservative Harold MacMillan and the Socialist Harold Wilson) in the 1960s.

But if the political parties refuse to discover latent public preferences, independent organisations can try to discover what can be discovered. (At least, they have not yet been suppressed.) And even if they have to use second-best methods that yield imperfect results, they can make available information on which a tentative judgement can be made about the claim of government to reflect public preferences.

Just as in 1963, 1965, 1970 and in 1978 the Institute of Economic Affairs used sample survey methods to discover how far the British people would prefer to pay for "public" services in the market rather than through government if they had a clear choice by not having to pay twice, so in 1978 it went further to discover how the British would like their taxes spent if they could not have them returned. The findings would provide a rough check on the existence of a social welfare function and begin to indicate how far government was reflecting public preferences, whether in public or private goods.

The findings were published in early 1979.[6] More than 70% thought government expenditure on one or more of a group of seven public goods and private benefits, together representing about ¾ of total government expenditure (defence, education, health care, roads, housing, unemployment benefit, retirement pensions) should be different from the proportion currently spent by government. This is a first attempt at an elusive social statistic, but it suggests severe doubt about the claim that British government faithfully reflects the preferences of the people whom it loudly and often claims to "represent."

VI. Cash Limits and Pricing Disciplines on Government

If government is not reflecting public preferences, and the solution is not, or not only, to control it by constitutional reform but also to reduce its province to public goods, how is the contraction to be achieved?

The revolt against the state has begun in the USA, in the California vote on Proposition 13 to limit local taxes. A modern Lenin might have argued, turning Marx on his head, that the people would first resist and roll back the state in the country where it had encroached most on personal/private lives. That country, apart from those like the Communist societies of Europe or Asia where rebellion is suppressed by force, is Great Britain. The British Welfare State, above all in education, medical care, housing and pensions,

6. *Over-ruled on Welfare*, Institute of Economic Affairs, 1979.

has invaded personal and family lives to a point at which resistance and rebellion might have been expected at any time since 1948. It is the Welfare State rather than nationalisation of fuel and transport that is now provoking rebellion, because technical/market conditions prevented the state from establishing complete monopoly. Nationalised coal has faced competition from private oil, and nationalised railways from private road and air transport. The consumer of fuel and transport has never felt so much at the mercy of a state monopoly as the consumer of state education or state medicine.

It was natural for the rebellion of the citizen against the state provision of personal/private goods to take the oblique form of resistance to high taxation. In Britain resentment against high taxation, or against particular forms of taxation, has historically provoked armed rebellion or constitutional revolution. Wat Tyler led a Peasants' Revolt against taxation from the English county of Kent in 1381; the Glorious (because bloodless) English Revolution of 1688 was a revolt against the powers of the monarchy, *inter alia* to tax. The American Revolution of 1776 was a declaration of independence from Britain because its Government did not sense how its colonial subjects would react to taxation. The bloody French Revolution of 1789 was stoked by unacceptable taxation. The epidemic of European Revolutions in France, Germany, Italy and elsewhere in 1848 were aggravated by the over-taxation of petty princes or provinces. The American tax revolt of 1978 was ignited by a rejection of local taxes in California.

Rebellions against taxes are not directly rejections of big government and its invasion of personal/private lives. Professor Milton Friedman has rightly assessed the California vote for tax limitation as encouraging but not adequate on these grounds. But, to the extent that government spending is limited to tax revenue, a vote against taxation is a vote against government spending, and therefore a vote for cutting government down and rolling back the state. Government may have income from trading; it can borrow; and it can inflate its revenue by printing money. And to the extent that the people limit its revenue by refusing to pay taxes, government may resort to all these three—and possibly new and unknown—methods of maintaining its spending power. But a vote to limit taxation is a natural first step in voting to limit the size of government. An electorate that has voted to limit taxation has warned government that it is not likely to approve expansion in government spending. A vote for lower taxes is not a vote for higher tax revenue.

In Britain changing public attitudes to taxation have been recognised by both main political parties, but they have thought mainly of spending limitation: "expenditure ceilings" or "cash limits." Here Professor Friedman has proposed defined cuts in expenditure of X per cent, with the tactical advantage that individual Ministers of Departments would be out-manoeuvred into disputing among themselves on how the total reduction should be divided among them instead of using their familiar tactics of justifying additional expenditure for themselves without reference to any of the others, which is invariably persuasive because additional expenditure brings a positive even if relatively small return. There is little doubt that this internal bargaining would be a formidable step in the effort to reduce the size and power of government as a whole.

Nevertheless the control over government that economists of the Austrian school would wish to urge, in addition to the "cash limit" approach, would be more market-oriented. To use terminology that not all liberal economists find congenial, the "cash limit" approach is macro-economic. The micro-economic approach would be to reduce the size of government by introducing prices for government-supplied personal/private services.

The micro-economic method would have three fundamental advantages over the macro-economic. Cash limits leave the decisions on slimming or "taming" government with politicians and bureaucrats. Pricing would transfer the decisions on cutting down, or cutting out, government to taxpayers/consumers. Even if, say, a 10% cut in the total budget were translated by political bargaining/trading between politicians and between bureaucracies into 15% in defence, 8% in law and order, 6% in health, 4% in education and 2% in roads, cash limits would entail the probability that government would use them to "cut" the highly-desired flowers as well as the dispensable weeds in personal/private services. Individual preferences may be, say, to maintain or even increase government expenditure on police and roads, which many people in Britain may wish, and reduce it on education and health care, leaving individuals to pay more for them privately. Cash limits are not likely to reflect individual preferences with such refinement.

Secondly, charging would make cutting government expenditure more likely than would cash limits since it would transfer the political unpopularity of reducing education, health, housing or other ostensibly desirable welfare services from politicians to the public. Professor Buchanan has pointed to the political unrealism of Keynesian "demand management": that it supposed politicians would be equally ready to create budget surpluses by raising taxes as budget deficits by cutting taxes. He argued that politicians enjoy spending and dislike taxing. *Pro tanto,* politicians do not enjoy announcing reduction in welfare (or other) services but, as Governor Jerry Brown of

Table 1. The Scope for Charging to Avoid Over-Government (Britain in a recent year)

	Percentages†	
	of total government expenditure	of gross national product
I. Public goods with inseparable benefits (charging impracticable or uneconomic)		
Military defence	10	6
Civil defence	*	*
External relations (embassies, missions, EEC, etc.)	2	1
Parliament & law courts	1	*
Prisons	*	*
Public Health	*	*
Land drainage & coast protection	*	*
Finance & tax collection	1	1
Other government services	*	*
	15	8
II. Public goods with some separable benefits (charging partly practicable)		
Government (central & local) and public corporation current & capital expenditure	6	3
Roads and public lighting	3	2
Research	1	*
Parks, pleasure grounds, etc.	1	*
Local government services (misc.)	2	1
Police	2	1
Fire services	*	*
Records, registration, surveys	*	*
	14	8
III. Substantially or wholly separable benefits (charging substantially practicable)		
Education	12	7
National Health Service	9	5
Personal social services	2	1

Table 1 (continued)

	Percentages†	
	of total government expenditure	of gross national product
III. Substantially or wholly separable benefits (continued)		
School meals, milk & welfare goods	1	*
Employment service	1	*
Libraries, museums & art galleries	1	*
Housing	9	5
Water, sewage, refuse disposal	2	1
Transport & communications	5	3
	40	22
IV. Subsidies, grants, pensions and other (mostly) cash disbursements		
Agriculture, forestry, fishing, food	3	1
Cash benefits for social insurance, etc.	16	9
Miscellaneous subsidies, grants, lending, etc. to private/personal sector	3	2
	22	13
V. Interest on National Debt	9	6
Total government expenditure	100	56

*Less than one per cent

† Details may not add to sub-totals because of rounding.

Source: *Charge,* pp. 46–7.

California has shown, learn to enjoy cutting taxes as soon as public opinion shows it wants taxes cut. Charging thus has political as well as economic advantages over cash limits.

Such a method of reducing government expenditure would be especially applicable in Britain, and its experience would be a guide to other Western countries whose governments have gone down the same road as the British but do not yet provide personal/private services on as large a scale, and to countries in the East which could be tempted to venture down the same road. A year ago I tried to estimate the scope for pricing ("charging") for British Government services (see Table 1) and emerged with the approximation that no more than one-third of all government services were public goods in which joint consumption made charging impracticable (or uneconomic because the revenue might fall short of the costs of collection) and no less than some two-thirds comprised essentially separable personal/private services for which charging was practicable, probably economic, and highly desirable.[7] What would be the comparable German, French, American or other figures?—probably much higher than in the market oases that have had unexampled rates of economic growth because their "public" sector is smaller, their bureaucracies fewer, and their taxation lower.

A third advantage of charging is that it is more likely than "cash limits" to prune personal/private goods out of the "public sector" and leave government with public goods. Taxpayer/consumers cannot, by definition, reduce their individual expenditure on public goods except by emigration. Charging would in time reduce the demand for government supply of personal/private goods, since charging for, say, formerly "free" state education, or charging a market rate for, say, formerly subsidised local government homes, etc., is tantamount to reducing the price of private education and housing. Parents and tenants would therefore raise their demand for private education and housing. In time, most personal/private goods would be transferred out of government into the market. And government would be left providing public goods.

VII. The West's Road the East Could Avoid

Western countries which have over-expanded government now confront, or before long will confront, taxpayer-citizens increasingly frustrated by government supply of personal/private goods. They have a choice of methods by which to extricate themselves from their error. Taiwan, Hong Kong, Japan and other market societies which have not yet over-expanded their government services can avoid the error by leaving personal/private services to develop in the market where they can be paid for directly by consumers with rising incomes. And for consumers with low incomes the solution is not to operate on the side of supply and provide these services by govern-

7. *Charge*, London, 1977.

ment without charge ("free") or at a below-market price, but to operate on the side of demand and "top up" low incomes by a reverse income tax or vouchers until incomes rise sufficiently to dispense with such temporary expedients.

The market societies in the East will be tempted by a plausible argument that was once dominant in the West, and still bemuses some politicians and bureaucrats, but has become discredited by events. It was that, as incomes rise, government can "afford" to spend more on social/welfare services. As argued above, the more valid principle is that, as national income rises, government should spend *less,* because an increase in national income implies that private incomes have also risen.

The danger in acting on the former Western fallacy of raising government revenue *pari passu* with national income is that government expenditure tends to rise faster than national income because it is politically easy to extract larger tax revenues out of people whose incomes are rising. This has been the experience of almost all Western countries, which have found their governments spending a gradually *rising* proportion of national income. Although personal expenditure has risen absolutely, it has fallen as a percentage of national income. And the process continues for decades, until taxpayers wake up to the truth that if their incomes are rising they do not have to pay higher taxes to enable government to provide them with services they can pay for themselves, with all the added advantages of choice between competing suppliers in the market.

The political difficulty of reducing government once it has grown large is again illustrated by the state of Tennessee, which, three months before California's Proposition 13, approved (by a two-to-one majority) an amendment to its Constitution to limit the increase in state government spending to the "estimated rate of growth of the state's economy," that is, its national income. This principle of raising government spending proportionately with national/personal income has been heralded as an historic victory of the people over government. Given the vested interests of politicians who love power, bureaucrats who love influence, and state employees (from teachers to firemen) who love their jobs, the claim is understandable. But it goes only half-way to the right relationship between government expenditure and national income. There is no reason at all why the first should rise faster or at the same rate as the second. The right relationship is *inverse:* expenditure should *fall* as national/personal income rises.

But it is more difficult to reduce than to enlarge government. And in the decades when government expenditure rises faster, or even at the same rate, as national income, rising taxation burdens industry, weakens incentives to work, acquire skills, train for management, take risk, start new businesses. All these qualities have helped build the economy and prosperity of Taiwan, Hong Kong and Japan, and their impairment could alter the general direction of effort, enterprise, growth, therefore income and standards of life, and so their safety and national security.

Of even more intimate concern for Chinese and Japanese culture could be the repercussions of the over-expanded state on family life. After 30 years of the Welfare State, both British political parties have "rediscovered" the family, and have belatedly recognised the alarming signs of its disintegration in the increasing births outside marriage, a high rate of divorce, juvenile delinquency, truancy and even arson in (state) schools.

Yet all these and more symptoms of breakdown of the family are not surprising when the state has interposed itself between parents and children. When the state supplies schools, parents feel they do not have much influence in their children's education, and children sense their impotence. When the state provides medical care, parents feel they cannot do much to help their children in sickness or accident, and their children do not look to them for help. When the state (or local government) supplies housing (as it does for one British family in three), parents are seen by their children as having almost no control over the conditions in which they live. And when the state provides pensions in retirement and generally takes care of old people, the bonds between parents and children are stretched, weakened and broken.

How the Chinese family, with Catholic and Jewish families among the most closely knit in the world, and the Japanese family (70 per cent of which have their aged parents living with or near them), would stand up to these strains is for Chinese and Japanese leaders to judge; and the people will judge them. It may be that they would stand up well. But there is no reason to subject them to the strains in the first place. On the contrary, there is strong reason for avoiding the strains by refining the market as the Taiwan, Hong Kong and Japanese economies develop, so that individual and family preferences can be expressed without the direct intervention of government, which can then concentrate its resources on the provision of public goods that their people want but cannot provide by private trading in the market.

Not least, the market oases of Asia could also escape the increasing corruption and rejection of the law evidenced in India and other countries in Asia that have tried to replace the market by government but have succeeded only in driving the open market "underground" into black or grey markets. The contempt for the tax laws in Southern Europe has lately spread to historically law-abiding Britain, where a new form of tax "avoision" has appeared: a mixture of tax avoidance (legal) and tax evasion (illegal) that expresses in the taxpayer's mind a blurring of the moral distinction between the two that used to be acceptable because it was thought that what was legal was moral and what was illegal was immoral.

This distinction has lost its influence on British public attitudes and behaviour. In the first place, there is something artificial and hypocritical in the distinction between tax avoidance and evasion if what is moral avoidance one year can be made immoral evasion in the following year by a change of mind among politicians or bureaucrats concerned with self-interest as much as with public well-being. Secondly, governments are not necessarily capable of moral behaviour solely because they represent majorities: sheer numbers do not transform immorality into morality. "Majorities," as Hayek says, "no longer even ask whether what they decide is just." Third, as recounted above, post-war British governments have not even represented majorities. Fourth, while government has a moral authority to tax all citizens to provide public goods, no such morality extends to taxes levied to supply private goods that taxpayers can arrange with less coercion themselves. Fifth, government which levies taxes that the populace indicates it resents by increasing "avoision" may be regarded as more immoral than the citizenry that avoids or evades them.

Such attitudes would spread in any society where growing government made necessary high and rising taxation. The East could not escape the economic consequences of high taxation experienced by the West.

VIII. Salute

Such are the lessons from the enlargement of the state that liberal economists using the market analysis refined by Hayek can teach the East to escape. In saluting his 80th birthday, the leaders and peoples of the market oases of Asia could be as much indebted to him as are the people of the West who are at last heeding his warnings against abandoning the market.

Summary

As incomes rise and become more equal in competitive societies, individuals can pay for more goods and services in the market: yet British government has since the last world war, and further back for a century, increased its supply. Some of the expansion has been in defence and other public goods, but most of it has been in private/personal/family benefits: education, health care, housing, pensions, transport, fuel, and other services. These tendencies have recently become evident in the market oases of Asia as well as in industrial countries of the West.

The nine arguments for expanding the government supply of goods and services—poverty, irresponsibility, equality of access, parity of esteem, economies of centralisation, natural monopoly, external benefits, external detriments, demand management—have been increasingly seen to be vulnerable and unfounded. But liberal economists could have used two general arguments against state supply: first, that the hypothetical case for government provision was at most an argument for experimentation, not for comprehensive national supply; second, that even if experimentation had indicated that state supply has advantages, they did not justify monopoly. To allow private production and distribution in the market was the only way to demonstrate the superiority of state supply. Exclusion of possibly superior private alternatives was too high a price to pay for the supposed advantages of exclusive state supply.

In practice, even in Western countries with "liberal" traditions, state supply has been increasingly exclusive and has led to deterioration in the quality of state services. The evidence is most clearly apparent in British medical care and education.

The extension in the Western democracies of state services from public to private goods has created unnecessary social conflict. The majority/committee procedures necessarily used by government have suppressed individual preferences. The resulting tensions and conflicts are increasingly seen in Britain. The existence of suppressed preferences is evidenced by field studies that demonstrate a wide gap between the small private sectors in medicine and education that are "allowed" to exist by the side of state medicine and education and the much larger market supply that would result from the creation of unbiased choice through reverse income taxes and/or voucher systems. These developments in Britain and in other industrial countries in Europe, North America and Australasia show undesirable economic and political consequences that the market oases of Asia could avoid.

State economy maximises group conflict and individual frustration; markets minimise them. Further field surveys in Britain suggest that the social welfare function was a figment of the state planners' imagination or wishful thinking.

The defenders of state supply have resorted to the false claim that democratic "representative machinery" can make it accountable to the citizen.

This machinery is less egalitarian than the market: the inequalities that arise in the market from inequality in income and wealth are less difficult to modify than is the inequality of cultural, "social," economic or political power which decide access to services in state economy. State "representative machinery" is usually manipulated by articulate activist individuals or groups, usually more literate and moneyed than the average, and is therefore inegalitarian as well as arbitrary and "unjust."

The further claim that public preferences are respected by the machinery of party politics in representative government is no more convincing. In Britain the party in government has not represented majorities of electors since the 1939–45 war; there has often been little or no choice between their policies; and there has been no opportunity for the citizen to record preferences on single services.

The task of confining government supply to public goods will require not only macro-economic "expenditure ceilings" or "cash limits." It will require also micro-economic market pricing or charging, which would be more refined in reflecting individual citizen preferences and be more certain to contract government since it would transfer unpopular political decisions from government to individuals in the market.

Taiwan, Hong Kong, South Korea and Japan have made the fastest postwar economic advance because they have based their economies on open markets and have, so far, avoided the errors of the West in expanding the functions of government from public to private/personal/family services. The recent advice reaching their governments from officials, academics and politicians that, as their national incomes rise they can "afford" to spend more on "social welfare," etc., is an error based on a misconception. There is still time for them to avoid it. The proper relationship between government expenditure and national income is not direct but inverse: as national income and therefore personal incomes rise, government expenditure should fall.

If the market oases of Asia follow the errors of the West they will confront new problems of resistance to government, a weakening respect for law in general, increasing tax "avoision," undermining of the family unit, retarded economic growth, decelerating living standards, weakening national security.

AVOISION

THE MORAL BLURRING OF A LEGAL DISTINCTION WITHOUT AN ECONOMIC DIFFERENCE

Avoision

The Moral Blurring of a Legal Distinction Without an Economic Difference

I. Introduction

The *IEA Readings* have been devised to refine the market in economic thinking by presenting varying approaches to a single theme in one volume. They are intended primarily for teachers and students of economics but are edited to help non-economists in industry and government who want to know how economists can explain their activities.

In recent years economics has extended its interests to subjects not normally thought to be within its province. Professor George Stigler of Chicago has described the process as a kind of economic "imperialism." Among these new subjects are charity, marriage, child "production," dying, riots and revolution, crime. Yet students of economics as taught at the London School of Economics, notably by Professor Lord Robbins, will know that since his seminal book, *The Nature and Significance of Economic Science,* in 1932, economics is regarded as an aspect of all human activity where the task is to allocate scarce means between alternative ends.[1]

Legal, Moral and Economic Distinctions

One of these new subjects to which economists have been giving increasing attention is tax avoidance and evasion. First, the *legal* distinction between the two is unambiguous: efforts within the law to minimise tax payments are described as tax avoidance; efforts outside the law to minimise taxes are described as tax evasion. Second, the *moral* distinction is, or was thought to be, equally clear. The normal law-abiding British attitude was

1. In 1948 Professor Ludwig von Mises's *magnum opus, Human Action,* showed the science of economics to be the study of human behaviour (praxeology) based on a unique approach to the nature of human knowledge (epistemology).

that what was legal was moral and what was illegal was immoral. Even then there has been a tendency to distinguish between the spirit and the letter of the law, and to regard as moral only that which conformed to the spirit. This judgement required the taxpayer to make the difficult distinction between the intention of the law and its consequences. But it tended, questionably, to regard as immoral forms of legal tax avoidance that frustrated the spirit of the law even though they observed its letter. These attitudes raise difficult questions not only about the intention of law-makers but also about the capacity of the citizen to interpret their intentions.

Third, the *economic* distinction between avoidance and evasion is almost non-existent insofar as the causes and consequences of tax avoidance are the same as for tax evasion. Clearly the economic causes and consequences are not dependent on the state of law, passed by possibly a bare majority of legislators representing a minority of taxpayers, since the law by retrospection can make illegal in the present what was legal in the past. Equally the economic causes and consequences of past laws could not be dependent on the subsequently unknown intentions of law-makers. A qualification here is that the causes and consequences may be affected by the duration of the tax laws, and so about the intentions of the law-makers and the prospects of reform. The consequences of a tax law regarded as temporary might thus be different from those of a tax law regarded as more permanent. The consequences might also be different according to whether it is regarded as desirable in the national interest or as politically motivated.

II. The Meaning of "Avoision"

The five essays in this *Reading* were assembled to explore the interrelationships between the legal, moral and economic aspects of avoidance and evasion.[2] The term "tax avoision" was coined to describe the emerging amalgam. (The alternative, tax "evadance," is less euphonious and less logical, since avoidance normally precedes evasion.) Tax avoision is thus used to indicate the blurring between tax avoidance and evasion that arises from the looser connection between the legal and the moral: it is tax minimisation with elements of both avoidance and evasion practised by the taxpayer who has difficulty in equating the legal with the moral and the illegal with the immoral. The parallel is with the attitude to rationing and other controls

2. Editor's note: This paper was first published as the Prologue to a book of Readings. See the Introduction to this volume, p. xii.

during the last war when, despite the common danger and the common loyalties it was expected to engender, evasion of rationing, etc., was always thought to be unpatriotic but was often the subject of banter or even social boasting by normally law-abiding citizens as well as by habitual black-marketeers. Many otherwise patriotic and honest people were not abashed to refer to the pound of sugar or the nylon stockings they were clever enough to obtain "under the counter." That was the consequence, even in a crisis of national survival, of trying to enforce laws that fell foul of the citizen's sense of acceptable restrictions in everyday personal life. How much less likely are regulations to be accepted and obeyed when the over-riding common national danger is absent.

III. The Extent of Tax Avoision

The extent of tax avoision would seem impossible to calculate. Although it is thought to be practised by people in all social groups, few would readily admit to it in public. It would therefore be impracticable to discover its extent by questioning the public. Yet if they would not indicate the *income* they received but did not report, it might be possible to discover the cash *payments* they made but also did not report. A small IEA survey in 1976 discovered that cash payments were made for a variety of services from architecture to house-painting. There is certainly a growing body of writing on tax avoision (of which an IEA *Occasional Paper* was an early pioneer).[3] Not least, the Chairman of the Inland Revenue, Sir William Pile, has recently suggested[4] that the income on which tax was evaded had so far reached 7½ per cent of GNP or around £10,000,000,000 (ten billion pounds). This is an average of rather under £200 per man, woman and child in the British Isles. The tax evaded may have amounted to between £3–3½ billion or about £60 per head. And, as it is presumably not practised by everyone, the average evasion per evader is even larger. The assumptions and calculations for this estimate have not been published and scrutinised. Other estimates may be higher or lower than Sir William's.

Anxiety about the extent of tax avoision is not new. In evidence to the Expenditure Committee of the House of Commons in 1975, Sir Norman Price, who preceded Sir William Pile as Chairman of the Inland Revenue, said about its extent and duration:

3. A. A. Shenfield, *The Political Economy of Tax Avoidance,* Occasional Paper 24, 1968.

4. In evidence to the House of Commons Expenditure Committee, reported in *Financial Weekly,* 30 March 1979.

> I think avoidance is growing and in my view it has become a national habit. Even if rates of tax were reduced quite considerably it would still go on.[5]

When asked by Mr. Nigel Lawson, now Financial Secretary to the Treasury, how he defined avoidance he replied:

> . . . the re-arranging of one's affairs in an artificial manner . . . for reasons only of avoiding tax. People tend to go a long way round to get at the same results as may be achieved by a much quicker route because by that long route somewhere along the way they can avoid tax. That is what I would regard as artificiality, the creation of the long route.

In reply to a question from a member of the Layfield Committee on Local Government Finance,[6] in 1975, a spokesman from the Inland Revenue said on the dis-incentives to pay taxes:

> We cannot tell how much tax is evaded—one cannot know the unknowable—but I think there are certain signs that now evasion has reached a point that is very serious indeed. . . . [W]e are back to something like the rate [of income tax] during the war for most people, which was regarded as very high indeed. There is, in my view, a serious risk of increasing the amount of evasion.

Results of Tax Avoision

Whatever the extent of tax avoidance and evasion, economists must study it as a growing part of economic activity that is not recorded in official accounts of national income, national expenditure, or national output. To that extent it conceals the volume of the national economic activity, the distribution of income, the distribution of factors of production between activities according to the ease or difficulty of tax avoision, the effect on emigration and immigration, and so on. Economists must also take into account the attitude of citizens as employers and employees, as spenders and savers, as producers and consumers; and all of them will be influenced by their attitude to the extent to which they distinguish between the legal/illegal and the moral/immoral aspects of tax avoision.

5. First Report from the Expenditure Committee, Session 1975–76; *Financing of Public Expenditure,* Vol. II: "Minutes of Evidence and Appendix," HMSO, 1976, p. 182.

6. *Local Government Finance,* Appendix 8: "Local Income Tax: Evidence and Commissioned Work," HMSO, 1976, p. 126.

To discuss these approaches and their inter-relationships we have assembled essays by an economist, Professor A. R. Ilersic of Bedford College, London, an authority in accountancy, Professor D. R. Myddelton of Cranfield School of Management, a sociologist, Dr. Christie Davies of the University of Reading, and two specialists in tax-gathering and administration: Anthony Christopher, the present General Secretary of the Inland Revenue Staff Federation, and Lord Houghton, a past General Secretary of the IRSF. Within their academic disciplines and spheres of experience they analyse the inter-relationships as they see them. They were given a difficult task since avoidance/evasion has only recently been examined by economic analysis.[7] The various strands in the argument are brought together by Dr. Barry Bracewell-Milnes, an acknowledged international authority on the economics of taxation and the author of several works, including a recent book,[8] that demonstrate his approach to the subject. Most observers have hitherto been more concerned to measure tax avoision and assess its consequences than to analyse its causes and possible cures. It is hoped, therefore, that the essays here will stimulate thinking by students of the subject in the universities as well as by practitioners in the civil service, the accounting profession, in industry which collects taxes, and by the general public which pays them.

Causes of Tax Avoision

The causes of tax avoidance and evasion are disputable. They range from a supposed general degeneration in moral standards to the increase in the rates of taxes since the war to meet expenditure evidently (and increasingly) not approved by taxpayers.[9] For economists, interest focusses on the extent to which tax avoision arises from the reduction in the net earnings from labour. Elementary economics would seem to suggest that, if the reward left to the labourer is reduced by taxes, he will labour less hard or less well. The difficulty is that there is both a price effect and an income effect. If the net earnings (price) are reduced by taxation, the supply of labour will fall; but if the labourer wishes to maintain an accustomed stream of income and standard of living he may work longer or better the lower the net price of each hour, week or month of labour. It has been found difficult to assemble evidence on the way individuals would react to changes in the rates of taxation of their efforts as measured by the tax on their final or "marginal" hour, week

7. The five essayists did not see one another's essays before publication.

8. *Tax Avoidance and Evasion*, Panopticum Press, 1979.

9. Ralph (now Lord) Harris and Arthur Seldon, *Over-ruled on Welfare*, IEA, 1979.

or month. Partisan claims are of little help: opponents of high taxation emphasise its disincentive price-effects; partisans of high taxation emphasise its possible incentive income-effects. Yet the partisans of high taxation have not so far made their case: it is not clear that the onus is on the partisans of lower taxes to demonstrate that they would encourage earnings. Despite the absence of evidence (apart from emigration), the advocates of high and rising tax rates are not decisively convincing when they claim that the dis-incentive effects are negligible. Lord Robbins has argued:

> I suppose that all but the completely unworldly would agree that a marginal rate of 100 per cent would have some adverse effects on the disposition to work or save of most ordinary people. Why then assume that the rates which actually prevail in the United Kingdom in the present day should not operate in the same way? Is it really to be supposed that the disincentive is absent until one reaches 99.9 per cent and then suddenly becomes complete?[10]

A comparable process is true at the opposite extreme. All but the completely unworldly might also accept that if the marginal rate of tax on earnings were reduced to nil, so that an earner could keep all he earned, the disposition to work would be heightened. The very growth in unrecorded work and earning, in which employers and employed take the law into their own hands and pay no tax at all, is itself telling evidence. There would be at least a shift back from unrecorded to recorded work. The conclusion would be all the more true if income tax were repealed for the second time, as it was first in 1816, and as it notionally could be if the state taxed only to finance public goods (below), its classical function.

Forms of Tax Avoision

The forms taken by avoision in everyday dealing indicate the anxiety to minimise tax payments and the ingenuity employed in minimising them. The most obvious is the replacement of cheques, which are recorded, by cash, which is not. Economists used to think that some 90 per cent of all (business and personal) payments in the modern economy were made by cheque and 10 per cent by cash. Payment by cheque is now almost certainly much less general. An increasingly common practice among suppliers of

10. *Political Economy Past and Present,* Macmillan, 1976, p. 116.

personal services is to indicate two prices: a higher one for payment by cheque and a lower one for payment by cash. A third and more extreme form of avoision is the development of exchange of services without the use of money in any form, in the return of mutual truck or barter, typified by the dental surgeon who accepts plans for an extension to his home as payment from his architect patient. Fourth, a form of tax avoidance that could lead to tax evasion (by cash payment of skilled assistants to amateurs) is the encouragement to do-it-yourself house repairs and maintenance and a host of other jobs the taxpayer can perform without paying tax in the fees otherwise charged by the professional supplier.

The "Subterranean Economy": Some Evidence from the US and Britain

Evidence for the increasing use of cash as taxes are raised has been discovered in the USA. Dr. Peter M. Gutmann, of the City University of New York, found the evidence in a study of the American economy from 1892 to 1976.[11] Despite the tendency for transactions to be paid by cheque as the economy develops, the use of cash increased relatively more than cheques from 1941 to 1945, when there was an increase in tax avoidance and of tax evasion in the black market. From 1945 to 1961 the growth of payment by cheque revived. From 1961 until 1976 payment by cash again grew more rapidly than payment by cheque as taxes were again raised under Kennedy and Johnson. He estimated that, by 1976, the subterranean economy had an "illegal GNP" of $176 billion (about £80 billion) and that rising taxes would drive more of the US economy underground. He concluded:

> The subterranean economy, like black markets throughout the world, was created by government rules and restrictions. It is a creature of the income tax, of limitations on the legal employment of certain groups, and of prohibitions on certain activities. It exists because it provides goods and services that are unavailable elsewhere or obtainable only at higher prices. It also provides employment for those unemployable in the legal economy; employment for those . . . whose freedom to work is restricted; and incentive to do additional work for those who would not do so if they were taxed.

Episodic or circumstantial evidence on avoidance/evasion in Britain was discovered by the chairman of a highly profitable and highly respected chain

11. "The Subterranean Economy," *Financial Analysts Journal,* Nov.–Dec., 1977.

store, Sir Marcus Sieff of Marks & Spencer.[12] He found that the branches with the best sales of some high-priced commodities were not only in areas with high official employment and high pay but also in areas with high *un*official employment, otherwise known as "moonlighting," or high official unemployment but with social benefits supplemented by earnings from unofficial employment. Shrimps at £4 per pound were selling well in Cumberland, Lancashire, Newcastle and Plymouth, despite high (official) unemployment.

> I wondered why our business was buoyant in these areas. . . . The conclusion I came to was that there is a bigger sub-economy in Britain than I ever dreamed of.

The anxiety to avoid/evade tax is seen in the loss taxpayers voluntarily suffer by refraining from shifting money from current to deposit bank accounts. Current accounts are not reported to the income tax authorities; deposit accounts are reported. Current accounts earn no interest, deposit accounts now earn around 9 per cent. Although the taxpayer would be better off if he transferred unrequired money from a current to a deposit account, the reluctance to pay tax seems to weigh even more. There could hardly be a more profound witness to the antipathy to pay taxes. Greater hate hath no man than this: that he cut off his income to spite his tax-gatherer.

Tax avoision affects the size as well as the distribution of the national product. According to whether it discourages or encourages work, it makes the total product smaller or larger than it otherwise would be. Insofar as it encourages the direction of effort into work where tax avoision by payment in cash or exchange of services is easier, it increases the income of people who happen to be endowed with the talents they can use in services where tax avoision is easier. Not least, by encouraging do-it-yourself servicing, it reduces the openings for specialisation, which Adam Smith taught was the fount of productivity, and thus arbitrarily both diminishes the national product and re-distributes it in favour of people who have a wider range of skills and away from those who are more specialised.

The Tax Avoision Industry

The growth in tax avoidance and evasion consumes hundreds of millions of man-hours and the talents of large numbers of men and women who would otherwise be contributing more directly to the national product.

12. *Financial Weekly*, 23 March 1979.

Moonlighting, Official and Unofficial Employment: A Two-Hour Untaxed "Own-Time" Working Session?

Evidence of the spread of moonlighting or other forms of unofficial employment reinforces and helps to explain the findings of the field survey (conducted by England, Grosse & Associates for the IEA) that there is a widespread and significant view which holds that over-time and other "out-of-office" work should not be taxed: over two-thirds of the sample (69 per cent) thought they should pay no tax at all "on what I earn in my own spare time."

■ This intriguing distinction in the public's mind between the acceptance of tax on official work and the rejection of tax on work done in "a man's own time" suggests a proposal: that the idea be applied to the working day with substantial benefit to the national income and to living standards even without anyone working harder or longer. (And if some did one or the other, or both, they would expand national income even further.)

■ It is a long time since the campaign of the 1820s and 1830s for a 10-hour working day. Whether or not it was premature, or too inflexible, whether or not it harmed individuals or raised national output, there might now, in 1979, be a campaign for a *two*-hour untaxed day, with no prospect of damage to industry or individuals, since the new working day would not limit but encourage work. If the public distinction between acceptable tax on official working time and unacceptable tax on unofficial working time continues, it would serve the national interest to divide the working day into two portions: a taxed portion and an untaxed portion.

■ The remaining official working day would yield more than enough taxes to enable the government to finance "essential" "public goods"—from defence to national parks. (It would thus be a new instrument in the hands of a government determined to "roll back the state.") The untaxed hours of the working day could then be arranged variously to suit the circumstances and preferences of individual employers and employees. The increase in national output would doubtless be very substantial. In total the number of hours worked per day might be eight, nine, ten, or even more.

■ Such a proposal would be supported by taxpayers in general and employees in particular. And it would suit employers. The engineering industry strike in 1979 for a shorter working day might be interpreted as a desire for a shorter *official* working day but possibly a longer *total* working day by making more time available for unofficial work. Thus, the government could accept that hours worked beyond 40, or 38, or 42, were official, untaxed "own-time."

■ The engineers cannot be condemned as the only group with these aspirations. There is now ample evidence, analysed by Professor Ilersic, that the wish to avoid and evade tax has been spreading into all occupational groups. The attitude to this aspiration should turn on the effect on the national income and living standards and, therefore, on the increased resources produced for generally agreed governmental "public" purposes as well as for private purposes.

September 1979 *A.S.*

These tax-recorders, tax-gatherers, and tax-hunters are employed both in government and in industry.

Tax avoision induces taxpayers to undertake expenditure on activities they might otherwise exclude. The effect is typified in this extract from the autobiography of Peter Ustinov,[13] a man of extraordinarily versatile talents who touched life at many points arising out of his career as an author, playwright, actor, film star, designer and director of plays, films and operas, as Rector of Dundee University for two terms of three years each, and not least in his activities in raising funds for the United Nations International Children's Emergency Fund (UNICEF):

> . . . my new adviser asked me . . . what kind of car I drove.
>
> "Aston Martin," I replied.
>
> "Oh God," moaned my tax-man. "Must you?"
>
> I answered with some liveliness. I told him London was full of even more expensive cars, Rolls-Royces and Bentleys. Who bought them? It couldn't all be inherited money. Or was it merely that these proud owners had had more imaginative advice?
>
> He grunted in a non-committal way, as though overflowing with bitter secrets.
>
> "All right," he said, "what other car have you?"
>
> "I have no other car," I answered.
>
> "Oh good God," cried the tax-man, now really upset.
>
> My first economy measure in the reconstruction of my parlous finances was, therefore, to go out and purchase a Standard Eight which I didn't need, as a personal car, so that I could put the Aston Martin down to business. I began to learn the nature of the cloud-cuckoo atmosphere in which we were beginning to live, and the gratuities as well as the price of freedom.

Mr. Ustinov offers two more examples of the unforeseen consequences of high taxation. As a tax exile, first in Montreux and then in Paris, he recounts entertaining instances in his reluctant absence from England.

> Our English accountant thought we were gone for a year, and I must say, so did I at first, but Suzanne [his wife] had other ideas. The recurring theme was Switzerland, and whereas I did not much care for the stigma attached by the press to the so-called tax refugees, I was sufficiently irritated by the greed of the British tax authorities when it came to those engaged

13. *Dear Me,* Heinemann, 1977; Penguin Books, 1978.

> in the liberal professions not to turn an absolutely hostile ear to the idea of emigration. I felt that, if successful, we were treated as little factories, and I thought then as I think now that the attitude was disastrously short-sighted and damaging.
>
> As always, there were many ingenious loopholes for those engaged in commerce—the South of France abounded with luxury cars with British registration and immense yachts at the times of the most draconian travel restrictions—and, since I spent less and less time in Britain anyway, it began to be a form of masochism to expose myself to the endless and ruinous inconvenience of acting as custodian for monies which would be confiscated, apart from the tip.

The third incident is hilarious:

> Naturally attention was already focused on Noel Coward and Richard Burton, brain-drain pioneers, today accorded the same grudging admiration as conscientious objectors. I was in Canada when I received a call from the *Daily Express.* A supercilious voice said: "Ah, Mr. Ustinov, there's a rumour going around town that you're about to do a Noel Coward. Is there any truth in this?"
>
> "You mean that I'm going to appear at Las Vegas?" I asked.
>
> There was an appreciative snigger, and then: "No. That you are actually going to set up house abroad."
>
> "Oh," I cried, as though my dull head had seen daylight for the first time, "you don't mean doing a Noel Coward, you mean doing a Beaverbrook!"
>
> His tone was hardened at the mention of his boss. "What exactly are you suggesting?" he inquired.
>
> "There's a rumour going round here in Canada that he's left to go to England. Is there any truth in this?"
>
> There was a pause. "Fair enough," he said, and hung up.

IV. Tax Avoision and the Public

Alternatives to PAYE

The possibility of reducing the costs of tax collection have led the Inland Revenue into an examination of replacing PAYE by other methods of collecting tax from wages and salaries that has a bearing on tax avoision.[14] It

14. Inland Revenue, *PAYE—Possible Future Developments,* Somerset House, March 1979.

considers methods of self-assessment, such as used in the USA, but argues that since it would be voluntary it would be more open to abuse and would require stronger sanctions. This view implies that taxpayers do not want to pay taxes to pay for the services supplied by government and would maximise tax avoidance and/or evasion. It thus raises the wider question of the attitude of taxpayers to the purpose for which taxes are raised.

If taxpayers consider that taxes are the payment for desired government services there would be less reason to suppose they would wish to avoid paying them. Even then, there would be the difficulty of government in obtaining payment for public goods that confer joint benefits on all, since each individual will wish to avoid payment for services he cannot be prevented from enjoying, and thus obtain a "free ride." There is now possibly a deeper doubt in the taxpayer's mind about the more personal government services. The Inland Revenue requires that expenses claimed for exemption from income tax shall be "wholly, necessarily and exclusively" incurred in earning. The even more far-reaching question is whether the taxpayer can regard taxes as raised by government "wholly, necessarily and exclusively" to pay for essential services. Examination of the structure of government services as they have developed, especially since the end of the war, seems to indicate[15] that only some one-third of total government expenditure is on joint public goods proper, and two-thirds is on cash transfers and separable personal services or private benefits that taxpayers could pay for in other ways—in which they could also command more authority by paying for them with a choice between competing suppliers.

It may be this increasing sense that money is being asked for by government for services that it does not have to supply, and that it supplies them less satisfactorily than they could be supplied in the market, that could help to explain the increasing reluctance of taxpayers to pay taxes. The evidence on public preferences between paying taxes for government services and paying prices in the market for private services is not easy to assemble, not least because it is necessary to build into the researches knowledge of the prices of government and private services with which most people will be unfamiliar; yet, despite the difficulties and imperfections, the evidence[16] seems to suggest an increasing desire since at least 1963 to pay less in tax and more in price for choice of services.

15. Arthur Seldon, *Charge*, Maurice Temple Smith, 1977.
16. *Over-ruled on Welfare, op. cit.*

Tullock's Analysis of Public Attitudes to Evasion

The relationship between the public approval or disapproval of government expenditure and their attitudes to tax evasion are discussed incisively by Professor Gordon Tullock,[17] one of the Founding Fathers of the modern economics of public choice:

> The individual presumably is interested in the taxes being collected from other people because he wants the government services that will be purchased by them. He would prefer to be left free to tax himself, but this is unfortunately not possible. In a sense, he trades the tax on his own income for the benefit he obtains from the purchase of government services by the entire community. It is by no means clear that for everyone the present amount of government services is optimal. If we felt that the total amount of government services being purchased today was excessive (i.e., that lower tax rates and lower levels of service were desirable), presumably we would feel relatively happy about systematic evasion of a tax law on the part of everyone. On the other hand, if we felt that the present level of government services was too low and the taxes should be higher, we might conceivably feel that "over-enforcement" is desirable.

Professor Tullock argues that, even if taxpayers approve of the existing volume (and, he might have added, distribution) of government expenditure, it would not follow they would favour efficient enforcement of the tax-gathering rules. If taxpayers thought they could avoid/evade taxes, they might prefer relatively high tax rates with low enforcement that permits extensive evasion to lower tax rates and stronger enforcement that brought in the same revenue. Most taxpayers, he argues, would nevertheless prefer the lowest rates of taxes for a given volume of government services, on the elementary ground that people prefer the lowest prices for given quantities or qualities of goods.

If this is the proper social goal, it is possible, says Professor Tullock, to deduce a simple formula for taxpayers' decisions on whether or not to avoid/evade taxes. If the amount they might have evaded multiplied by the probability of avoiding detection exceeds the fine payable on detection multiplied by the chance of detection, they would logically attempt evasion. This

17. Richard B. McKenzie and Gordon Tullock, *The New World of Economics*, Richard D. Irwin, Illinois; Irwin-Dorsey International, London, 1975.

economic calculation of the "profit" or "loss" of attempting evasion implies no moral judgement.

Not least, the method of gathering taxes may affect taxpayer attitudes to avoision. PAYE, invented by a temporary bureaucrat for war-time convenience, is in a sense an "impertinent" tax that does not allow the taxpayer the dignity of paying tax but deducts it from his earnings before he receives them—rather like the high-handedness of solicitors who deduct their costs from a client's receipts from sale of a house or compensation for a loss and send their cheque for the balance. Here again, the taxpayer may put maximisation of revenue second to the satisfaction of receiving the whole of his pay packet and paying taxes on request. The taxpayer would then know more vividly how much he was paying and relish the authority of paying it. A tax withheld is a tax yielded with less grace than a tax paid by overt act.

Will Tax Cuts Change Habits of Avoision?

Whatever the legality, morality, or economics of avoidance and evasion, and whatever stronger penalties and powers government may take, avoision has been spreading so far that it may be difficult to control except by removing the initial impetus of the increasing taxes which generated it. William Pitt's purpose in reducing customs duties in the 1790s was largely to reduce smuggling, corruption and worse; and in some measure he succeeded. The question is whether the habit of avoiding and evading tax as it has developed in the 1970s will be easy to break once taxes are reduced, or may have become irreversible. Sir William Pile says that avoidance would continue even with large tax cuts. It may be that the Italianisation (or Swedenisation?) of the British fiscal system is either here to stay or will take a long time to be dispersed by the re-assertion of the traditional British respect for law which successive British governments have now evidently strained too far.

William Pitt wanted to reduce indirect taxes in order to raise their yield. He surmised that lower duties would cut, or cut out, smugglers' ill-gotten gains and be more effective in wiping out smuggling than severe enforcement by revenue officers or by savage penalties. Lower duties, he thought, would affect both supply and demand—they would reduce the financial inducement both to buy smuggled goods and to sell them. In time the smuggling, and the violence and gang warfare it generated, declined. In our day there can be little doubt that tax avoision has increased with the increase in taxes of recent decades, so there must be strong reasons for supposing that tax avoision will fall away if taxes are lowered enough. This conclusion cannot be established by field research or other evidence, but it follows from the common observation of human nature which underlies the economist's law of demand that the lower the price the higher the demand and the lower the supply: so the smaller the gains from avoiding/evading tax the less there is likely to be.

Adam Smith's Four Canons

Pitt's policies on taxes, designed to ensure that they minimised evasion, fraud and costs of collection, were in part inspired by Adam Smith and his celebrated four canons of taxation: equality (in the sense of equity to reflect individual ability to pay), certainty, convenience, and economy. Smith said:

> Every tax ought to be so contrived as both to take out and to keep out of the pockets of the people as little as possible over and above what it brings into the public treasury of the state;

it should not require

> a great number of officers;

it may

> ... discourage the people from applying to certain branches of business which might give maintenance and employment to great multitudes;
>
> it may frequently ruin ... by forfeitures and other penalties ... those unfortunate individuals who attempt unsuccessfully to evade the tax;

it should not

> subject the people to the frequent visits and the odious examination of the tax-gatherer [and so] expose them to much unnecessary trouble, vexation and oppression. . . .

Adam Smith's canon of "certainty" (that taxes should be paid by the people intended) is possibly the most elusive of the four to satisfy. A general difficulty with taxation as a method of financing services is that it is almost impossible to discover who eventually pays many or most individual taxes. The task of identifying the taxpayer rests on the economist's distinction between impact and incidence. Legislators usually cannot proceed much beyond identifying the taxpayers on whom the taxes are levied, but they do not know where their taxes ultimately come to rest. The initial "impact" is often little guide to the ultimate "incidence." The tax buck is passed on from stage to stage in economic relationships. If the demand for a taxed product is elastic, the producer who is taxed cannot pass any or much of the tax to the next stage; if the demand is inelastic, so that buyers will go on buying if the tax is added, it will be passed on. A tax on petrol can ultimately be paid by disabled drivers. The uncertainty of taxes partly or largely impairs one of Adam Smith's four canons, and makes all taxation systems precarious as instruments of government policy. Thus taxes ostensibly levied on companies may in the end be paid by unsuspecting individuals. "Soaking the rich" may end in robbing the poor.

If tax avoision is on the scale indicated by Sir Norman Price and Sir William Pile, and if it produces unrecorded activities that would not take place if tax had to be paid on the earnings they produced, a delicate issue is whether the law, even if it could be (expensively) enforced, would be enforced at too high a cost in lost output. Like the elimination of environmental pollution, the suppression of tax avoision may be bought at too high a price. Yet, if this is true, high taxes will have provoked diminution in the respect for the rule of law that may have lasting repercussions elsewhere throughout British public life and private morality. The dilemma is that an ounce of tax avoision may still be worth less than a ton of national income.

V. The Economist and Tax Avoision

The economist's approach to tax avoision is different from that of the lawyer, the moralist or the administrator. The difference is fundamental. It was formulated forcefully by Professor J. M. Buchanan, with whom Professor Tullock has worked closely:

> The economist's stock-in-trade—his tools—lies in his ability to and proclivity to think about all questions in terms of *alternatives*. The truth judgement of the moralist, which says that something is either wholly right or wholly wrong, is foreign to him. The win-lose, yes-no discussion of politics is not within his purview. He does not recognise the either-or, the all-or-nothing, situations as his own. His is not the world of the mutually exclusives. Instead, his is the world of adjustment, of co-ordinated conflict, of mutual gains.[18]

18. "Economics and Its Scientific Neighbours," in Sherman Roy Krupp (ed.), *The Structure of Economic Science: Essays on Methodology*, Prentice-Hall, Englewood Cliffs, N.J., 1966, p. 168: quoted in McKenzie and Tullock, *op. cit.*, p. 1.

And on the specific issue of tax evasion, the task of the economist is to calculate an "optimum" tax enforcement policy that would optimise not only tax revenue but also all the other objectives that the citizen would consider desirable, and which, at the margin, he might prefer to optimising taxes: take-home pay, production, privacy, income to alleviate poverty or others.

Tax Enforcement

An even more delicate issue is that of tax enforcement. It was said to be an objection to the 1971 Industrial Relations Act that it envisaged penalties, including imprisonment, for sizeable numbers of trade unionists if they broke the trade union law. Edmund Burke's dictum: "I do not know the method of drawing up an indictment against an whole people" is no less relevant in the enforcement of tax laws. There are some 35 million taxpayers, including around 20 million in PAYE, compared with 12 million trade unionists. If tax avoidance and/or evasion is as widespread and as tenacious as the Inland Revenue Chairmen have reason to believe, enforcement seems a formidable burden on government. If taxes are paid unwillingly, the taxpayer may find ways to keep himself two or three steps ahead of the tax-gatherer. Although it may seem sensible to proceed by sample prosecution as a lesson to the rest, there is even here an element of arbitrary justice. And if avoidance/evasion is on a large enough scale to warrant more extensive prosecutions and sanctions, Adam Smith's apprehensions about "unnecessary trouble, vexation and oppression" may come to be shared more widely.

These are some of the issues that are far from being resolved in the academic analysis and public discussion of the blurred amalgam of tax avoidance and evasion that I have called avoision. They will no doubt require long exchanges between economists, sociologists, accountants, tax-gatherers and taxpayers before they are finally resolved, short of lasting and irreversible damage to the British economy and society.

THE DILEMMA OF DEMOCRACY

ACKNOWLEDGEMENTS

I have to thank mainly my teachers at the LSE in its heyday in the 1930s, who rose above the faith in the state of its founders Sydney and Beatrice Webb.

In the writing of *The Dilemma of Democracy* I am indebted to all my teachers and friends, and especially three who prompted the book or offered suggestions.

John Davey, formerly Editorial Director of Blackwell, suggested, after *Capitalism,* a study of democracy, of which this is a condensed version.

My economic history teacher in the Sixth Form at Raine's Foundation School in the East End of London originally warned me of the dangers of the state by lending me his student notes on the English Guild system and mercantilism.

And Professor David Conway suggested caution in my forays into philosophy, and especially reminded me of Hobbes's *Leviathan* that caused me to respond with Benedict de Spinoza.

A.S.
July 1998

INTRODUCTION

Escapable Government Meets Irresistible Markets

After the publication of *Capitalism* (1990), Blackwell had suggested a sequel on the anxieties I had there expressed on the fate of political democracy. It had been exceeding the domain of government acceptable to the people as evidenced by their widening disrespect and failing readiness to finance it. And their evidently growing disaffection could be traced to their increasing ability to escape from its tightening regulations, deteriorating services, and high tax-costs.

The State Is Rolling Back (1994) comprised 54 essays, since my student days at the London School of Economics, that traced the disappointing tendency of political democracy as it has developed in Britain to generate over-government and its failure to create the essence of democracy: rule by the people.

These doubts had crystallised by the 50th anniversary in 1997 of the Mont Pélerin Society of international liberal scholars, where I ventured to argue that "the rule of law" in democracy had not created "rule by the people."

"The rule of law" is the covenant of the Western philosophy of liberalism which teaches that the essence of human progress lies in the libertarian process of liberation from restriction whatever its source. This is the political system that facilitates the art of individual learning from experience by taking risks in the unknown. For too long individuals in the Western world have been prevented by over-protective political authority from learning the lessons. Political authority had ended in stifling the freedom to learn. That lesson has in principle appeared to have been learned in the West. But not in practice. Political authority continues to suppress the individual learning process by over-government.

This Paper identifies the dilemma or flaw in the future and fate of democracy and its government.

Economic and political trends since 1990 have reinforced the sense of impending failure: that if democratic politicians did not withdraw their government from over-expanded services and rising taxes to pay for them the people would escape to spontaneous exchange and mutual enrichment in markets. If the rule of law did not underwrite the new freedoms to escape over-government, rule by the people, the essence of democracy, would be established by other means.

Conventional notions on replacing over-government by "limited" or "minimal" government seemed inadequate or unlikely. More fundamental thinking on the desirable and likely powers of government in the years ahead appeared long overdue.

For at least some decades ahead, government seems unable to withdraw to its acceptable limits. Its powers to order economic life will be increasingly by-passed where they conflict with the new opportunities opened by fundamental change in the conditions of supply and demand.

This approach differs from ingenious theories (explanations) of government that have attempted to reveal its origins, nature and extent. The title to this Introduction indicates the tension between political power and economic impulse expressed in the natural world impasse of "immovable objects meet irresistible forces."

Capitalism had argued that the government created by democracy in Britain since the last third of the nineteenth century had been growing far beyond its indispensable functions. It had enveloped the four groups of "public goods," "public" utilities, "social" services and local government functions that had been conventionally, but as the twentieth century developed prematurely, accepted as the desirable and indispensable province of government.

The classical catalogue of "public goods"—defence, law and order, and lesser functions such as local roads—had been thought since Adam Smith to be necessarily supplied by government. The "public utilities"—transport and power, water and drainage—were judged to be monopolies best left to the care of the state. The wide range of personal and family "welfare" services, education, medical care, housing and "national" ("social") insurance against interruptions in income, were gradually enlarged into a "welfare state" within the democratic political state. And local government had developed services extending from plausible "public health" precautions through libraries for the aspiring working man to luxury swimming pools, tennis courts and golf courses.

These "public" services and functions contrived to create the main impetus and justification for over-government. They have erroneously earned the endorsement of political historians. Belatedly, a counter-development in everyday British life has pointed to a different—smaller and diminishing—role for government. But it has been analysed less intensely by British historians and sociologists.

The neglected historical trend taught otherwise. Early private means of supplying welfare and "public" utilities that had emerged and developed in the nineteenth century were spreading in the early twentieth century. The trend grew more rapidly after the 1939–45 War, and has grown with unprecedented pace in recent decades and years. Rising private incomes in the past 40 years are now offering historically superior alternatives to the outdated but politically entrenched functions of the over-government generated by democracy.

The development least expected by conventional historians who recorded events without envisaging the likely alternative trends emerging outside government has been the multiplying new avenues of escape from over-government. The tax payments increasingly required by democracy were for services found to be inferior in quality and higher in cost than the competing offerings from outside the state.

Two sources of tension in state services demonstrate the dilemma. Teachers have had to be told by a Secretary of State for (state) schooling, more than a century after its establishment, that they must learn to teach the elements of education that are widely and well taught in private schools. The "managers" of the state's health services have been told by a Secretary of State that they may be charged at law if they fail to provide statutory standards of service in their establishments. Both Ministers sensed the urgency of improvement but continued their long-held faith that it can be provided by the democratic state.

Government is no longer universally seen as the indispensable sole supplier of goods and services requiring around half of national production and earnings.

It now appears increasingly likely that, if current British government does not systematically withdraw from many or most of the state functions created by its political predecessors, two consequences will be unavoidable. Further escapes to new suppliers outside the state will be sought. And payment—by taxes or other charges—for the superfluous activities of the state will be withheld.

This is the dilemma facing British, and Western, democracy. Its historic predicament is insoluble unless it accepts the logic of its weakening role in twenty-first-century society. But it may have left its withdrawal too late. If it does not freely allow recourse to better alternatives outside the state its functional ability and moral authority to administer the remaining indispensable "public" services will dwindle. And it will expose society to the very disorder it was created to prevent. The civic and productive order that democracy was designed to provide will provoke the disorder that Thomas Hobbes foresaw in his seventeenth-century *Leviathan.*

The question is whether democratic government has failed to see the significance of economic advance. It may have delayed too long the looming withdrawal to its historic role. Its fate is to relinquish the dispensable functions that it cannot maintain from diminishing resources. Its alternatives are order or disorder. If it does not withdraw in good order, by respecting the new abilities and aspirations of the people to escape, it will withdraw in disorder.

If it attempts general withdrawal it will incur widespread displeasure and probably social discord from its beneficiaries, increasingly its remaining employees. But if it maintains its functions it will have to contend with falling revenues from consumers who can escape to better services from a widening range of competitors.

The (so far seven) identifiable sources of over-government are reviewed in Chapter 2 and the (so far eight) escapes from over-government in Chapter 3. Both seem likely to be strengthened in the coming century.

Recent trends indicate that it is too late for a British government of any political party to continue raising increasing revenue to pay for the growing services it mistakenly thinks future generations will expect it to supply. If any ironic warning signal is required to discipline government's traditional expectations, it is its latest efforts to raise revenue from practices that British democratic law has blessed with legitimacy. The prospect of pursuing and persecuting taxpayers for (illegally) evading taxes that are (legally) avoidable must make it risk both the respect of its citizens and, more powerfully, their tax payment.

If legally avoided taxes are required to pay for dispensable state services the solution is to change the law in the legislative assembly to transform legal avoidance into illegal evasion. But the main result is likely to be increasing tax evasion, as is now evident from Europe (Chapter 3).

But that is the risk that government requiring more tax revenue must take. If government cannot persuade citizens not merely to obey the written law but also to respect its unwritten *intentions* by treating (some) legal practices as "antisocial," or by interpreting the intended new "spirit" of its laws, it is inviting widespread lawlessness. The claim of democracy to live by "the rule of law" will then lose its legitimacy and could dissolve into ridicule.

In the 1990s economic, technological and political trends have combined and accelerated to weaken the case for the unremitting government regulation of private and family life. The conditions of both the supply of and the demand for many or most of the four groups of government services have been changing more fundamentally than ever since the early nineteenth century. And the changes have decisively strengthened the ability of citizens as both voters and taxpayers to question the persistence of over-government.

The likely changes are clearly visible. By the early years of the twenty-first century the people will be able to reject much or most of the functions of government formerly accepted unquestioningly. There will be increasing debate on all four categories. "Public goods" in defence, law and order, art, culture and heritage will have to justify themselves as necessarily state functions. The "public utilities," from transport and power to refuse collection and prison administration, misleadingly labelled as necessarily "public services," will be seen as better organised outside government. The large group of personal welfare services will be seen as better supplied by non-bureaucratic agencies. And most local services will be—are being—better supplied by competing suppliers.

Historians may once have overlooked or understated the early beginnings of many "public" services in the 30–40 years of economic liberalism in the mid-nineteenth century. Some are rewriting history.

For the first time in British history since the century of state education from 1870 the new British Government has rejected the characteristic fallacy: that exclusive state control was necessarily the ideal objective. In January 1998 it recognised that it could learn from private education by inviting its advice. If in education, the lesson and the same revolution in political thought will before long have to be admitted in all the main welfare services since they all embrace the same fallacies.

The gradually spreading reactions of people in all social groupings have generated resistance, as consumers or taxpayers, both to the intrusion of the state into private lives and its over-regulation of working lives. In the archetypal public goods there is general acceptance of private suppliers of functions traditionally regarded as the province of central or local government. In public "utilities" the private companies in rail and road, gas, electricity and water, are accepted, not without criticism but with expectation that inadequacies are likely to be removed sooner in competitive markets.

In the "social" services all four main categories of "welfare"—education, medical care, housing, and insurance—are losing parents, patients, property-owners, and potential pensioners to private suppliers. There is expansion in private schools, private medical insurance, home ownership despite the period of negative equities, and not least private saving, despite the early over-selling. And local government cannot compete with flexible firms in supplying most urban and rural services.

That the long-outdated faith in "public" service survives is seen in the latest government proposal for local authority home property valuations to prevent "gazumping" in house purchase. Politicians in all parties still do not understand the market. Free markets cannot work if their essential mechanism, the ability to offer varying terms until contracts are signed, is suppressed. The next logical step for this outdated purpose would be to put *all* privately-owned homes into local government control as with the five million council houses and tower blocks that few children of their tenants will want as "homes" in the coming 10 years.

The change from the long-standing state supplier to new private competing suppliers is for most people a new experience, especially the older people who unquestioningly accepted the state services as irreplaceable.

Wider choices have soon freed lower-income consumers and shoppers from sole dependence on government sources. And as producers and earners they can now increasingly redirect their everyday working and earning, buying and selling, saving and investing from the monopoly of the state to the wide range of private competitors. Their interests had been slowly moving from dependence on government from which there was no escape to a range of suppliers that could be rejected if their services deteriorated. There is still no escape from a wide range of government suppliers, from the General Post Office (Royal Mail) for most letter postage to local council housing with millions of "captive" tenants.

A more unexpected post-war trend has reinforced the lessening dependence on government goods and services. The increasing reluctance of the people to provide in taxes as much as government demands is still not understood by politicians as the growing power of the people no longer dependent on them for most of their services.

The resulting stringency in government revenue has not yet been seen as reflecting the emerging public mood of resentment and rejection. The historic motivations range widely: from the eighteenth through nineteenth century rejection of desirable taxes by smuggling and other blatant law-breaking, to late-twentieth-century doubt about the much larger government levies, and now in the coming twenty-first century increasing suspicion that government services cannot be as good "value for money" as the competing private services.

The latest scholarly researches into the likely reasons for tax rejection

(Chapter 3) suggest fundamental public reaction against the weight and complexity of taxes. And the extensive regulation of economic life has come to be seen as a main cause of the illegal "evasion" that may now have to be accepted as a wide reaction to the excesses of over-government.

The change in the relationship between government and the people is fundamental to the prospects for democracy. Its representative parliamentary government is no longer seen as the natural, historic, benevolent, sole provider of essential services. It has become a competitor with numerous independent suppliers who have to be more sensitive to individual requirements, expectations, and aspirations.

The state is also increasingly resented as rapacious in its demands for a large share of the people's earnings. And it is no longer accepted or feared as the only source of essential services since the dawning realisation and evidence that government cannot simply command payment by law.

The "rule of law" has been weakened by excess, by extending its activities where the people believe they are better judges than government and its agents, however well-intended they may be. The rule of law can no longer express the opinion of government on how society should behave. If the people can withhold payment of taxes government must be more sensitive to the sensibilities of the people.

The resistance to the 1980s "poll tax" was provoked by the failure to explain that it was a collective tax-charge for local services. Price-charges for personal individual amenities, especially such as tennis courts, swimming pools, or golf courses rarely used by the lower-income ageing residents, would have been more acceptable. The 1997 Government has removed charges for art galleries and other "cultural" amenities on the ground that cultural education must remain "free," which means paid for by taxpayers who may not visit them, and who will search for compensating legal avoidance or even illegal evasion. Government has yet to learn that unnecessarily collective "charging" for personal services that can be paid for by individuals who use them are resented by people who do not. The citizen will always be a step or two ahead of the slower-moving tax bureaucracy.

The new public attitude to taxes marks the deterioration in democracy brought by over-ambitious political leaders. Academics who have long taught that government, composed of selfless, public-spirited saints and seers, must replace the market, must have by-passed the newest branch of economics, "public choice," that studies politicians as individuals who are no less self-interested than the people in whose name they govern. The persistent error, one of many underlying the continued faith in government, has been to suppose that individuals appointed as public servants have been transformed into public benefactors.

The politicians, ill-advised by academics, have ignored the historic conception of democracy as "rule by the people." They have over-reached their role as servants of the people, overestimated their benevolence, and persistently ignored the seismic changes in the economy that undermine its failing claim to the loyalty of the people.

The long-term changes in the fundamentals of the supply of "public" services and the demand for them have been obscured by the preoccupation of government with the short-term importunities of the organised interests whose universal plea of "underfunding" begs all the questions. Government reactions required to meet the higher standards in goods and services offered by private suppliers too often end in wasteful emergency expenditures, as in patching state schools, National Health hospitals, council homes that will before long be repudiated by the younger generations, and local government services they will condemn as extravagant.

The clearly implied warnings of changing public mood and expectations have been misunderstood or underestimated in political and public, and more surprisingly, academic debate. The interminably rising public revenues demanded by the state have been weakening the mutual trust and respect between government and people on which democracy rests. Yet to maintain its straitened sources of government revenue, democracy is now reduced to the dangerous extremity and historic risk of pursuing taxpayers accused of failing to pay taxes that the courts have judged they are not legally liable or obliged to pay (Chapter 3).

The traditionally law-abiding British citizen is now escaping from the costs of government over-regulation of economic life by recourse to the most ancient as well as the most recent forms of payment that minimise or escape detection. The most primitive, barter, was the earliest trading method, followed by "cash" in valuable metals or "worthless" paper, and most lately electronic money and a return to pure barter in the exchange of goods and services without the use of money of any kind.

Combinations of payment can be used in the wide extremes of transactions: from face-to-face exchange to trading on trust with unknown strangers who become allies and friends, not least on the postal or voice mechanisms of the Internet. These are the new world-wide exchanges and trading with mutual benefits between strangers in the universal markets created by the power, identified by Adam Smith, of self-enrichment to enrich one another.

By the 1970s there had been disturbing public disapproval of government encroachment on family efforts to raise living standards. For 30 post-war years the welfare state had employed paternalistic and maternalistic provision, supervision, regulation and admonition in the elemental individual and family requirements of everyday life. Resentment and resistance were stirring. At the Institute of Economic Affairs a new word was coined in 1979 for a study to examine whether, in times when government judged it essential to remove 40 to 50 per cent of the public's earnings, it seemed that the taxpayers' legal minimising of taxes and their illegal rejection of taxes might be inter-related. *Tax Avoision* was the title chosen for a collection of essays by academics and tax specialists to reconsider the economic, legal and moral inter-relationships between "avoidance" and "evasion."

The legal distinction seemed indisputable. The law had proclaimed that practices to reject taxes were either legal or illegal. That established judgement has now been questioned by governments short of revenue and unable to borrow. But the economic and moral differences were less clear.

The formerly unambiguous legal distinction seemed to be obscured by differences between tax-gatherers and taxpayers on the interpretation of the law. The distinction was dangerously blurred in the November 1996, June 1997, and March 1998 Budgets. The anxiety of government to raise revenue by treating legal practices as illegal has stampeded it into weakening the rule of law. The basic economic effects on the production of goods and services might be much the same in the "official" legal and the "unofficial" illegal economies. The ironic effects on final real incomes, on the extent of poverty and the degree of inequality in incomes, might be even more economically advantageous in the "unofficial" than in the "official" economy (Chapter 4). Not least, the moral question required judgement on whether the tax-gatherers were levying more taxes than required for the amount, quality and cost of their "public" goods and services.

The moral question remains. Government may be thought eminently righteous in raising the revenue required for its functions delivered "in the public interest." It may also be judged unrighteous in levying more taxes than the taxpayers think its goods and services are worth. In the market this practice is called "over-charging." And sympathy lies with the "over-charged" payer rather than with the "over-charging" supplier. The difference is that unacceptable government "public" goods cannot always or easily be escaped by transferring the tax-payment to a competing supplier.

Earlier at the IEA, in 1963, it was thought time to reveal the error in opinion polling over nearly 20 years since the war which persisted in claiming to show that large percentages of national samples—approaching 80 per cent—were ready to pay higher taxes for higher expenditure on state services, especially welfare. Such surveys have continued to appear into the early 1990s.

The simplistic error was obvious to the economist. The samples were not being told the essential information of price—how much in taxes was required for how much more (or better) education, medical care or other services. The crucial information in the economic analysis of supply and demand was simply missing. Without it no taxpayer can answer such questions.

This micro-information, crucial for individuals, cannot be supplied by government, which deals in huge macro-totals. But it is routinely supplied every day in competitive private trading. When prices were introduced into the Institute surveys in 1963, and periodically over 24 years to 1987, the normal rational result emerged: individual taxpayers would spend more for government services if their tax-prices were lower, and less if tax-prices were higher. The higher the tax-price the lower the demand, the lower the tax-price the higher the demand. And, when the tax-price was reduced to nil for "free" services (or when it was concealed by having to be paid indirectly as taxes), the demand was infinite.

These were the state services that their suppliers accurately but confusingly complained were perpetually "under-funded."

When prices were openly stated in the unique Institute surveys it was possible to calculate the degree to which the readiness to pay higher taxes varied with the tax-prices of state services (the price-elasticity of demand) and to attempt a broad measure of the extent to which it varied between higher- and lower-paid income groups (the income-elasticity).

The neglect of price in the familiar opinion polls was, and remains, a surprising failure of judgement in the academic community and a weakness of British public debate in judging the public acceptability or rejection of high and rising taxes. The continuing absence of attention to the extent of the apparently increasing reluctance to pay taxes, which has acquired a long list of labels from "black" through "informal" to "underground" economy and several more, must now be given a morally neutral label to exclude unfounded moral prejudgement. The "parallel" economy is a description that does not judge how far the propriety or impropriety, morality or immorality, lies with government or people. It is a neutral measure of the various methods of payment and exchange of goods and services, including barter, to arrive at the resulting amount of production, distribution and exchange that takes place alongside the activities and transactions paid in the conventional or customary methods.

The importance of a measure of such "unofficial" activity is that, because its full extent is unknown, it is generally overlooked or understated in official government estimates of total national production, distribution and exchange. The understatement of economic activity is, moreover, aggregated in international totals, such as those of the OECD. World statistics published by government are therefore mostly seriously misleading: they understate production and incomes, saving and investment, and overstate unemployment and inequality, poverty and deprivation. In short, they make judgement of long-term trends in economic and social life in countries and continents severely defective. For the subject of this study the conclusion follows that misleading opinion polling had encouraged the political parties to expand their over-government to the stage at which its unnecessarily tightening regulation of economic life and high rates of taxation had blindly distorted national and private lives.

Government lacks knowledge of the possibly wide gap between the immediate "impact" of taxes on its targeted or intended victims and their eventual "incidence" on strangers whom government cannot trace—buyers or sellers, employees or shareholders, savers or investors, importers or exporters, rich or poor, nationals or "foreigners." The so-called "social justice" of high taxes was among the more questionable consequences of post-war over-government.

From its early years the Institute had reacted against the failure of the universities to scrutinise the economics of large sectors in all four categories of over-government. It promoted early studies of the most neglected welfare services: pensions in 1957 and 1960, housing in 1960, medical care in 1961, education in 1964. "Public utility" studies began with television in 1962, followed by fuel and transport in 1963, telephones in 1966, North Sea gas in 1967, petrol and other fuels in 1969, and coal in 1974 and into the 1980s when previous governments' failure to adjust coal-mining to changing costs precipitated a minor "civil war." Among the so-called public goods, studies of financing local public goods services came in 1963, national public goods in 1964, with studies of defence and crime prevention in 1974.

All four classes of over-extended services had been largely ignored in the 20 years of gradually increasing over-government after the war. And they had largely escaped critical academic scrutiny until the Institute's Hobart (and other) Papers from the late 1950s questioned government policies and provoked academic, public and political alarm. But government learned slowly. The civil service and industrial obstacles to reform were tenacious. Little wonder that state expenditure financed by taxes expanded almost unnoticed for a further 15 years to the late 1970s.

The most fundamental questions in political economy, many largely evaded in political, public and even academic debate, were raised in these Papers. Yet the expansion in state expenditures was, even into the 1970s, and now in part into the 1990s, defended on the ground that some state services were new and required time to justify themselves. But there were also other neglected effects. Private competing production was inhibited. And government had no information on which to base its claims that its services were superior to all possible alternatives. The disturbing political truth is that post-war British democratic government for a third of a century from 1945 to 1979 felt safe to continue its unquestioned expansion until the belated reaction in the early 1980s and perhaps now again in some forms in the late 1990s.

The continued inflation of government frustrated the most fundamental precepts in the political economy of liberal society. Among the most fundamental recent misconceptions have remained the error, in effect taught by the political class, that government can be the source of righteousness—justice, compassion, equality, and, among the most question-begging, "fairness," "decency," and other such undefined offences against the English language. Government has been presented by the politicians of all parties as the all-merciful god of democracy.

The debilitating historic truth that will have to be learned to explain why democracy cannot satisfy its repeated political promises is that its government has grown too large to command the economy by its laws, rules and regulations. The humbling lesson for politicians is that their power to do good or evil is increasingly subject to the private decisions of the people as individuals, families, and private groups and associations of all kinds in everyday buying and selling.

Democracy conceals a fundamental conflict in the efforts of the people to make the most of their abilities and aspirations. Their choices as voters between political principles, policies and sentiments at infrequent elections conflict with their fundamental real preferences as consumers who know costs and pay prices in everyday economic life. Whatever they may have been misled to hope from generous or myopic government they have been slowly rediscovering for themselves, by personal disappointment of state services, performance or promises, the truths of classical liberal philosophy. They are rediscovering that they themselves best know their powers and failings in private exchange of goods and services. And their choices can be made more effectively by the conventional or the newly spreading unconventional means of exchange.

The option is no longer for politicians to tell the people what they will do in government but to confess what they cannot do. The question for the future is increasingly not "What *should* government do now?" but increasingly "What *can* government do?"

As the people escape from over-government the risk for democracy is that it will not long retain the respect of the populace. This is the sobering fundamental state of political economy that should preoccupy academic, public and press thinking.

The conclusion reached here is that democracy can do no other than withdraw from its over-expansion.

The question is whether it can reduce its insatiable demand for resources and taxes to the amount approved and willingly financed in time to prevent final disillusionment with democracy.

The best hope lies in the early progressive reduction in the power of government over everyday economic life. The required reduction in its appropriation of national income is from over 40 per cent to nearer 20 per cent.

There are enough escapes from over-government for the people to be able to end its long tolerance of over a century. And the escapes multiply from day to day. The political parties can no longer convince the people that they will reject their servitude to long-loyal political supporters, organised allies, public officials, industrial federations, professional associations or trade unions.

The solution in principle is to confess the historic defect of democracy: that, despite its claim to respect the freedoms of the people, it generates too much government. Over-government is the historic defect of the political systems that have dominated economic life: not only socialism in various guises but also the social, liberal, or Christian democracies that claim to practise "limited" government.

Few democracies, the nearest perhaps Switzerland, have attained the "minimum" government that confined itself to the functions that the people cannot perform for themselves. Minimum government required it to allow the emergence of maximum market. No democracy can claim to have accepted the limitations of its powers by changing economic conditions.

The ultimate truth and the unavoidable but so far ignored conclusion is that the best hope of preventing the certain excesses of over-government is to prepare for the risks of under-government. And that requires individuals to be allowed in open markets to insure against the risks they should be able to run without obstacles from state over-regulation and over-taxation.

That minimal government with maximal market would entail risks of under-government is the essential difference between over-government and under-government. An indispensable element of reform is to return the judgement of risk from the political process, where it is chronically over-estimated by politicians anxious to enlarge government, to the informed experience of individuals, families, fraternal groups, common interest in everyday private life who bear the consequences of their misjudgements but who learn from experience how to judge and to minimise risks.

The transfer of power from politics to people requires private incomes and expenditure to be raised by no less than a third from 60 to 80 per cent of total national resources. The changed balance of expenditure between people and government from 60:40 to 80:20, halving the "take" of government, would create the main prospect of rebuilding "the rule of the people" in "the rule of *acceptable* law" by guarding against the persistent tendency of democracy to create chronic over-government.

CHAPTER 1

Democracy at the Crossroads

The Government of Democracy

The failing government of democracy, the results of its over-expansion, and the persistent inadequacies of its constitution are three political weaknesses that remain unresolved.

In the government of democracy no method of representation has yet been discovered to fulfil its historic promise of rule by the people. The Greek "demos," people, and "kratia," rule, provided the name but not the reality of "democracy" as it was envisaged down the centuries.

The "direct" democracy of assemblies in public squares for debating and voting as in the ancient Athens of the century 400 to 300 BC remains a mirage when government engineers its mandate once in four years to take powers over the details of human life. The "indirect" representatives of the people, debating and voting in legislative assemblies, produce régimes of political masters rather than servants.

The English civil war between the royal house of the Scottish Stuarts and the Parliament of largely English burghers in the seventeenth century left the common people with little political power. The reluctant yield by the aristocracy of the vote in the 1832 Reform Act began to give some political voice to some of the people. Yet political power to elect representatives was less effective in spreading self-rule by the people than was economic power of spontaneous exchange. Open markets developed strongly from the late eighteenth and early nineteenth centuries precisely because they were largely free of political control. The political liberties of the spreading franchise cautiously enlarged by Parliament in the mid-1800s were more securely ensured by the emerging freedom to use rising incomes for everyday food, clothing, and shelter and later for the early forms of private education, medical care and other welfare services.

For 30 more years from the 1870s until the late nineteenth century and then into the twentieth century economic freedom would have raced ahead of the still slowly widening political franchise. The spontaneous aspirations of the lower-income people enabled them to buy mutual and commercial "industrial" insurance against sickness, unemployment, old age and the other risks of life.

But the political franchise, although widened to women and younger people in twentieth-century democracy, was overwhelmed by the state suppression of the slowly growing economic freedom to buy services wherever they were available in developing markets of competing suppliers. Not the least were the "welfare" services of schooling, hospitals, the beginnings of home-purchase and assurance of income in the absence of earnings.

The illusion that it was the widening political franchise and representative Members in Parliament that created "rule by the people" persists to this day. The truth is almost the opposite. Accelerating advance in the underlying economic freedoms and choices of personal and family life have been overwhelmed by the abolition of choice in the services supplied by government, not least those described by the political euphemism "welfare." From the later years of the nineteenth century the people could freely buy food and clothing, beer and tobacco, fuel and transport, but were prevented or discouraged from paying directly for schooling, medical care, or insurance. Henceforward they lost the bargaining power of consumers who paid prices (school fees, insurance premiums) and were reduced to recipients of "free" services. The irony that many of them paid by taxes was lost in the history books.

Yet the most widely accepted definition of "democracy" persists in the vision of Abraham Lincoln on the battlefield of Gettysburg in 1863. *First,* it promised democracy by three apparently powerful controls by the people over their faithful servants in the Congress: government would be of the people. *Second,* it would be government by the people. And *third,* there would be government for the people.

None of these visions has been realised. It is too rarely observed in political histories of democracies that, in the original Greek of "demo-kratia," none of Lincoln's three promises of rule by the common people has been fulfilled.

The political history of the 135 years since 1863 has failed to produce the kind and size of government that creates the required democratic institutions. No democracy, certainly not in Britain, represents even indirect government of the people, the whole people, and nothing but the people. The people have diverse, often incompatible, hopes. No single form of democratic government can create the variegated political framework or environment for diverse life-styles, or accommodate the variety of human preferences. No democratic government allows small groups of minorities to accept or reject its rules and regulations, laws and taxes, and to live as they wish, even where diversity to suit individuals, small groups and minorities is feasible. The notion that its services are for "the good of the people" where the people could have services that suited diverse circumstances and preferences, is political fiction.

The failure of "democracy" is evident most fundamentally in the overused principle of majority. Because it seemed to offer the promise of "rule by the people" majority decision has been applied both where it is unavoidable and disputably beneficial as well as where it is patently superfluous and clearly undesirable. Because they seemed serviceable in a small range of services, the so-called "public goods"—public "utilities," elementary welfare services, and local government services—they were enlarged to cover much of personal and family life where decisions could be taken by individuals, small groups and voluntary associations.

The majority power of democracy is the source of arbitrary rule. Political democracy represents some of the people more than others. Majorities are not only potential tyrannies; they are also often irrelevant, inefficient, domineering, wasteful, intrusive, outdated.

Political democracies based on majorities are encounters of specialisation in political skills. Not the least offensive to the notion of "rule by the people" is the ability to create pressure on government that yields very much more to the organised than to the unorganised.

The result is a fundamental weakness in the creation of liberty. Democracy has yet to evolve the solution for its central weakness: that the more some people can organise to attract general public attention or sympathy the more they derive advantages or concessions, benefits or subsidies from government at the expense of others who lack the requisite skills. To speak of majoritarian democratic "rule by the people" is a careless distortion of the English language.

The fatal readiness of democratic government to yield to public pressure has stimulated the formation of politically-motivated organisations guided or managed by professional organisers to create the "lobby" operating in the wide range of interests from industry, the professions and labour to art, the theatre and sport. They have become a more influential and remunerative profession than university scholarship and its scholars who bestow untold benefits to all the people for untold generations.

The crucial damaging criticism is that the lobbies organise more effectively as producers than as consumers. And producer organisation is easier in longer-lasting staple industries or services—manufacturing, mining, rail transport, teaching—than in shorter-lasting, rapidly changing technology-based trades where individuals make five to 10 changes of employers or industries in a working life.

The even more fundamental human dilemma escapes detection by political analysts. The conflict of interest is not merely between industrial function. It is more essentially a conflict within each individual. Preferences and aspirations are essentially of the personal psyche. Democracy has performed the most unexpected disservice to individual coherence. It has incited many or most people to put their immediate, often temporary, interests as producers before their more fundamental long-run interests as consumers.

In political democracy as it has grown each man, and increasingly woman, is induced to organise against himself and herself. Each is induced to join other producers to extract advantages or concessions from government at the expense of their deeper personal interest as consumer. The conflict is between immediate and eventual interests. The advantages or concessions that raise the price of the product of each man or woman as a producer emerge as costs to him/her as a consumer. And the advantage or concession in a government subsidy for the production of a commodity or service benefits some individuals as producers but eventually injures every individual as a consumer and a taxpayer.

There is a safeguard against such political distortions, but it is a remedy that democratic government has chronically avoided or rejected. The safeguard is to disavow the power of government to grant advantages or concessions. And the institution that most forcibly incapacitates myopic government from such destructive temptation is the open market. This is the only mechanism known to human beings with the unique capacity to restore power to the people by denying it to their supposed political "representatives" in government. The market enables the people to express their decisions directly and more powerfully than in the legislative chambers of politics. And it is rarely understood that the market emerges spontaneously to remove its defects or "imperfections" if it is not suppressed by political power.

If the emerging working classes of England had been less seduced by the power to vote for the Liberal and Conservative politicians from the 1860s, if they had demanded freedom to continue building their private schools, hospitals, homes, and social insurance, they would have exercised more influence over their family lives and avoided the eventual capitulation to the disabling social legislation. And the army of "social workers" would not have had to be the instrument of a government-dominated environment that has debilitated the family and created much of contemporary social disorder.

Government has not been "of" the people. Neither is democratic government rule "by" the people. Nor is it government "for" the people. It has changed from its supposed nineteenth-century rôle as an avocation for the wealthy into the twentieth-century profession that commands high financial or other rewards for its skills of political organisation, management of elections and exercising power in government.

Democratic government cannot react sensitively to the widely varying circumstances of the people. It serves the kind of people who are most tenacious in manipulating the arts of "politics." Their causes, from the open interests of industry and agriculture to the disguised "disinterests" of culture and heritage, the arts and crafts, displace the good of the dispersed people who are relegated to a minor place in the queue for political preferment.

The Penalty of Over-Expansion

In recent decades democracy has inflated its powers too soon, too far and too long. It has created over-government even in the two or three recent decades when it was becoming patently even more superfluous.

Its services are now increasingly obtainable from other suppliers with higher quality and lower cost at home and increasingly overseas. And the people, aided not least by science and inspired by the will to be free, are slowly learning to escape from what must more truthfully be re-christened unrepresentative over-government (Chapter 3).

The escape is becoming too widespread beyond the power of democratic government to suppress. The historic "social contract" between benevolent accountable government servants and their masters, the sovereign people, was ostensibly for the ready payment by taxes for functions and services unobtainable from other sources. This supposed political settlement has been remorselessly dissolving.

What politicians maintain as the necessary costs of government are increasingly sensed as unnecessary costs of "over-government." And its taxes, originally seen by William Pitt as income tax, and accepted for a few years as payment for a good bargain, are being subconsciously but finally resented as too high for the quality and relevance of services available at lower cost and higher quality from competing suppliers in the market.

The gradual and imperceptible change in the attitude of the historically law-abiding English is seen in the too-little-studied evidence of the European and world-wide growth of diverse forms of tax rejection (Chapter 3).

The historic change in the growing disenchantment of the people with the rôle of government is explained less by the political scientists' analysis of representative institutions, or by the sociologists' preoccupation with the failure of government to satisfy "needs," than by the economists' analysis of the contrast between the decreasing value and the rising cost of government, not least in welfare. The political vote of approval by majorities, hitherto the political test of "democracy," has become less significant than the economic vote of rejection of over-priced government by the people as consumers.

The vital difference between the power of the people as voters and as consumers is too rarely analysed by the proponents of large functions for the democratic process. The voter is the victim of ignorance; the consumer is endowed with unique knowledge. The voter has to accept the intentions of government without evidence of past performance or the power to reject the results of years of power misused. The consumer is equipped with experience of personal wants and the immediate or early power to reject unsuitable suppliers.

The conventional and continuing contrast between benevolent government and rapacious competitors has been revealing in its lack of understanding of the relative power of the voter and consumer. The recent overselling of saving and pensions schemes was discovered over the years by the very existence of alternative suppliers and the power of the misled to withdraw and move between competitors. The misdescription by successive Governments of the British "National" Insurance Fund or "social" insurance as a fund accumulated and scrupulously invested to yield income for payment of sickness, unemployment or retirement "benefits" was known to Ministers and civil servants for decades but not openly confessed.

The people's choice is not between political saints and commercial sinners; it is between politicians who cannot easily be unmasked or escaped to redeem life savings and businessmen who unmask one another and can be abandoned with manageable loss.

Numerous avenues are opening for more people, especially down the income-scale, to escape from expensive, poor-quality, oppressive "over"-government that democracy persists in supplying in its "public" services (Chapter 3). The most fundamental escapes are the rising real incomes of the lower-paid and the lower costs created by advancing technology in competitive industry. The least studied are the changing attitudes to the payment for government and the new escapes again evolved by new technology.

The rejection of the historic acceptance, significance and sovereignty of government has widened in recent decades from negligible to substantial. It has been changing in subconscious stages from resigned acceptance of the political machinery to determined rejection.

Historically the legal avoidance of payment for "public" services has merged into technically illegal evasion and provoked further avoidance that cannot be redefined as illegal. (The relationships between legal and illegal rejection were reviewed above.) The citizen's efforts to minimise payable taxes by changing, reducing or entirely abandoning sources of earnings, not least by early retirement, are beyond the power of democracy to prevent—except by the involuntary labour that British democracy is dangerously approaching.

The leading responsibility for the diminishing respect for democracy and observance of its governing processes is that of the politicians. Even when well-meaning they are misled by the political scientists who have overestimated the beneficence and intention of democratic government. Political leaders have been interminably invited or incited to expand government, its powers, functions and services, beyond their necessity, beyond their innate low quality, and, not least for the lowest-income families, beyond their sheer cost.

By "cost" the economist supplements the everyday sense of financial payment by the more subtle economic sense of the sacrifices suffered, the alternatives that could have been produced and enjoyed but have been often wantonly lost. But the alternatives in more satisfying services that could have been supplied by a more diverse competitive structure of producers and suppliers are rarely discussed by British political scientists or sociologists.

Too little has been studied in the social sciences of the better-quality and lower-cost unknown alternatives—the public goods, the "public" utilities, the personal welfare services and the local authority amenities—that could have been produced for the people in place of the standardised, impersonal, unresponsive services rationed by government.

And too little has been written, even by specialists in fiscal economics, of the money costs to individuals and families. Government proclaims and publishes statistics of its high spending on "public" services. Totals with arrays of noughts to reach millions and billions mean nothing to individuals. The fog of figures without individual identity is pursued even into small areas of England. A county town in South-East England proudly informs its local taxpayers that it is spending on local services apparently huge sums expressed in macro-economic millions and billions that, to repeat, mean nothing to individuals.

Yet government is reluctant to reveal the individual micro-economic cost of each service for each service that would enable individual tax-paying citizens to compare the costs of government with the prices of suppressed competing alternatives—from home or abroad (Chapter 4).

Ignorance of cost and price has been compounded by the widely-used expedient of the concealment of price disguised as "free" supply. It began in the nineteenth century as a gesture of compassion for the poor. It degenerated in the twentieth into the most disabling obstacle to comparison of costs of government and private services. In the twenty-first century it may yet become an instrument of secrecy that will further weaken respect for democracy.

The expansion of "free" government services since the 1939–45 War was all the more untimely since it came in a period of rising real incomes ignored by government. It typified the temptation of democracy to base its policies and institutions on the receding dying past rather than on the evolving beckoning future.

The extension in 1948 to medical care of government service without payment was presented as the only means to ensure that the people would be provided with treatment when sick. It was an enlargement of the illusion that services requiring scarce equipment, labour and land could be "free" of costs and prices. Yet price is the sole measure, imperfect but unique, of the scarcity of resources and thus of the husbandry required in their use.

The government supply of "free" services has not miraculously abolished their cost but hidden and destroyed the best available measure of the care required in its use. And it was a further barrier to the comparison of government and competing services.

"Free" government services have acquired the potential of concealing from the sovereign people the alternatives that government can deploy to disguise its political purposes. That government may announce, with pride, that it has transferred £x billions to the National Health Service from other services, without revealing costs and values to individual consumers and taxpayers, conceals the only significant measure of the sacrifice of other services.

Knowledge of price induces the precaution of "thinking twice." The destruction of knowledge in "free" services induces irresponsibility. The 1997 Government sensibly seems to wish to use markets in some industries, but several Ministers seem to misunderstand the twin effects or results of knowing prices. Markets operate with—and reveal—"income-effects" and "price-effects."

The error has encouraged government to emphasise the beneficial "income effect" and ignore the discipline of the "price effect" of its measures. The removal of the income-tax rebate on private health insurance reduced the income of the supposed middle-income retired insured subscribers but raised the resulting price-effect that has induced many of them to return to the long waiting lists in the "free" National Health Service. And by making the lower-income retired patients join the waiting lists for medical care it has intensified the inequality in the long waiting it thought to reduce.

The mismanagement of "income-" and "price-effects" emphasises the misuse of political power that is now increasingly understood by the people as voters. But democracy will no longer be able to maintain over-government by controls or regulation that are increasingly doubted by the people as necessary or unavoidable.

The dilemma of democracy, hitherto widely neglected by its defenders and critics, has been that it must before long choose between opposites—withdrawing from its over-government of economic life and enforcing it by suppression of the escapes that are opening out. But, more fundamentally, if, as it increasingly seems, it has left the withdrawal too late, its fading resources may require it to replace over-government by under-government.

The 1997 Government has gamely seemed to be attempting both new regulations and relaxations. Withdrawal requires more fundamental rethinking, but would achieve more than suppression. The argument developed below is that withdrawal is becoming unavoidable if democracy is to retain its popular support or tolerance. So far it has not adapted itself more promptly to social and technological advance. Its future now turns on its readiness to shrink its economic domain, perhaps by as much as a half. If it fails, it faces the even more formidable prospect of waging guerrilla financial war against the people.

The signs of reality vary from the constitutional to the politically pragmatic. The most menacing, for democracy itself, are the efforts to outlaw the legal practice of tax avoidance. The latest is seen in the move against the sale of duty-free goods in the single market of the European Union, universally regarded as its most desirable achievement.

Government initially confronts both a dilemma and a new unknown future. If the escapes from its laws and taxes continue to accelerate, the future of political democracy in which the people as voters elect representatives will fade. Its future will lie in a new democracy based on the power of the people as consumers with power in markets for which government operates the rules required for observance of contracts.

These conclusions are documented and refined below.

The Disabling Constitution of Democracy

Democracy is weakened by four central fallacies in its claim or intention to serve the people who elect it. *First,* despite its pretence or intention to take the long view of the effects on the people of its government policies, it is essentially and unavoidably short-term in its political thinking. Government is elected or re-elected at the most in Britain for five years, for four years in the USA, for three years in Australia. But economic life continues for decades. No politically conceivable reform—even seven-year parliaments—can enable it to benefit the people in the long term by its wisdom or avoid harming them by its blunders. So they are passed on *après la déluge* to their opposing successors. And both engage in the political tactic of blaming each other.

Party A assails Party B for its "18 lost years" of 1979 to 1997 and "13 wasted years" from 1951 to 1964. In the responsibility of all parties for the political myopia of the post-war years, Party B could have blamed Party A for the "six backward-looking" years of 1945 to 1951, the "six drifting years" of 1964 to 1970 and the "five feeble years" of 1974 to 1979.

Five-year fluctuations in political decisions can disrupt the economic fluctuations over the still roughly 10 years average of the economic cycle between advance and retreat. Moreover, the political decisions of government can affect economic life for the much longer "secular" periods of up to 30, 40 or 50 years for which firms invest large sums in the production of goods and services to reflect their estimates of the long-term trend in demand for their output.

A *second* weakness compounds the first. Much though the two main political parties differ in their thinking and philosophies, and condemn each other across the floor of the House of Commons, both support the parliamentary system in which the alternating power of majorities predominates in *après nous la déluge* decisions.

This implicit "conspiracy" against the people is yet another fundamental flaw in the British constitution rarely discussed by the political scientists. For this abuse, as for others, of the political power of democracy the ultimate solution lies in reducing or removing the over-expansion of government.

The *third* weakness of democracy intensifies the conflicting economic and political cycle and the informal conspiracy between the parties. British (and other democratic) governments have the awesome power of patronage to favour individuals and groups: individuals by appointments, influence, monetary awards, titles, and groups in firms, industries, professional associations, trade unions, by subsidies, patents, copyright, preservation of existing jobs, suppression of competition, "protection" against imports, and more. Yet no politician has the strength to handle such awesome powers and resist the temptation of abuse. The few who have done so, like the scholarly Keith Joseph, have lacked the steel to enact measures they learned during opposition were in the long-term public interest.

The readiness of government to favour vocal organisations encourages the creation of the "pressure groups" that have become almost an accepted institution of political democracy.

The result is to restrain what would otherwise have been a much faster rise in living standards in the half-century since the last war. And that would have brought a more rapid removal of poverty, a faster reduction in avoidable inequalities, perhaps a halving in the real unemployment in the country as a whole by the readier movement from older to newer industries.

The political motivations of government in favouring production over consumption reverse the natural order of human preference to produce what people want as consumers rather than tamely consume what industry has produced. It thus distorts the structure of industry and the pattern of employment long after its periods of office.

The unavoidable conclusion is that the democracy that is supposed to express the wishes of the people ends by frustrating them because the legacy of government outlives it.

The political submission to established interests and the subjection of consumers to producers is seen most clearly in the persistent failure of government to empower low-income parents to escape from the worst state schools. The teacher trade unions virtually dictate the closed market of "their" (tax-paid) schools by opposing comparison with fee-paid schools. Yet comparison and judgement by parents could be arranged by allowing parents to transfer the cost of state schooling to schools they prefer. The voucher is increasingly used to create selection between alternatives. Its use for meals, books, and other purchases is teaching the potential power of choice in schooling that could end the disliked social divisions and create the "one nation" that politicians claim to champion.

The obvious logical way to end poor schools is to empower working-class parents to escape from them. That government has failed to put parents before teachers—consumers before producers—is the characteristic weakness of democracy.

The federal structure of the United States has enabled several states in the North-East to experiment with the voucher's means of escape. With varied experience the more workable methods are being discovered. And among their strongest supporters are black as well as white organisations of lower-income parents.

There can be little doubt that, despite opposition from the American teacher labour unions, the voucher system will spread into more states as the "public" (state) schools continue to fail. Among its advantages, which could be reproduced in Britain, is that competition from the private schools would raise the standards of the state schools.

A *fourth* weakness of democratic government as practised so far is that it distorts small shifts in public voting sentiment into large differences in Parliamentary seats and majorities. Since the last war winning parties with small, medium, and large majorities have claimed fundamental revolutions in public philosophy justifying massive reconstruction of economic life. Key industries in transport and fuel were made government monopolies. Voluntary initiatives were further depressed, especially in welfare. Local government activities were inflated. Little wonder the unguarded remark of 1945, "We are the masters now," has echoed ominously in 1964, 1970, 1979, and now in 1998.

The first post-war (1945) Government claimed to have acquired authority for expanding the state. The following Government of its opponents (1951) made the historic error of continuing this pretence. The accumulating over-government misled British democracy into over-estimating its politically moral authority.

The over-government that was begun too soon, was also extended too far, and is being continued too long (Chapter 2). Only now in 1998, after half a century, has democracy begun to acknowledge that the welfare state formed in the post-war years has outlived its day. The 1997 Government has bravely begun a tortuous task of "modernisation" that will be resisted and may be derailed by its "barnacles" (below).

Yet its thinking so far is half right and half faulty. It is high time to limit cash payments to low-income recipients. This course, urged in IEA Papers in the 1960s (Introduction), was confidently condemned for 35 years by all political parties and their academic advisers. A clear error now is to put more taxpayers' money into fundamentally flawed services—not least schools, hospitals and housing—that will soon be neglected and rejected.

But the political purse is not guarded as tenaciously as the private pocket.

No post-war government has been given a "mandate" by the "ruling" electors to revolutionise the legal-political framework of the British economy and society. The electoral system in 1997 again distorted the relationship between the voters' sentiments and their weight of representatives in Parliament.

The theory of representative democracy—that it creates "rule by the people"—implies that a change in the number of votes for a political group will produce a broadly comparable change in the weight or influence of their representatives, since legislation is decided by their votes. The 1997 Government that obtained 44.4 per cent of the votes has the weight of 60 per cent of representatives. Previous governments exerted similar contrasts between national sentiment and the power of government to change individual lives. Abraham Lincoln would not now endorse "government of 31 per cent of the people" (44 per cent of the voters).

The distortion in the *quantity* of representatives moreover distorts the influence of the *quality* of the competing arguments. Whatever the competing quality, the Government can by sheer weight of number create the legislation it has designed. The 1997 Government cannot be blamed for continuing the excesses of the political system that elected it. But it is not the democracy of "rule by the people." Nor is any other form of numerical representation, whatever the ratios of representatives to people, even if the number of representatives varies proportionately with the number of votes. The drawback, much sensed in Holland and elsewhere in Europe, is then that the voter loses personal touch with his representative. Quantitative proportional representatives can reflect public sentiment less than the qualitative personal knowledge of unproportional but known representatives.

There is no known system of political democracy by indirect numerical representation that ensures "rule by the people." Not least it compounds the error that majorities are "democratically" empowered to ride roughshod over minorities. The flawed theory of the precedence of majority over minority is the alleged justification for its use as the best method for measuring opinion on supposedly unavoidable "public goods" that create benefits for all. Elsewhere, in all other goods and services, interest lies in the minorities who require more refined methods of discovering individual and group preferences in families and voluntary organisations.

The "democratic" political system of deciding government policies by majority voting fails where many or most of its government services are provided for minorities with variegated preferences. The solution lies in the economic mechanism. That is the advantage of the market over the ballot box—whether in general or by-elections, in referenda or plebiscites.

In Northern Ireland hope lay in replacing military by political solutions. The April 1998 political agreement may require the reinforcement of the further market solution that enables minority Catholic families more influence in their choice of privatised schools, housing and other welfare services.

The form of democracy most likely to reflect the wishes of the people decentralises decisions where possible to private individuals or groups. The persistent use of the ballot box, and its enthronement of large groups, has caused embittered social friction and discord wherever it is applied (Chapter 2).

But even the ballot box may fall into desuetude. If political decisions are influenced by organised interests to the extent that discussions and decisions are made outside the legislative chamber and in the corridors of stately homes or urban organisations, the outcomes may be too late for the political representatives of the people to influence. Little wonder that the House of Commons has been sparsely attended except on exceptional occasions. And if the representatives who are to ensure "the rule of the people" are increasingly absentees playing political truant, so may be the electors from the ballot boxes at coming General Elections. They will find that decisions and signals to producers are more effectively made in competitive markets.

CHAPTER 2

The Debilitating Disease of Over-Government

Over-Government — Too Soon

Markets are imperfect because they work with and for imperfect people. The instinctive reaction of social scientists is to meet "market imperfection" by government "correction." Their error, even subconsciously, is to suppose that since the purpose of government is to correct error in the market, its well-intentioned performance must initially be supposed to be free from imperfection. Few social scientists are ready to concede that government may be more imperfect than the market. Yet the evidence of history is that the imperfections of government are more deep-rooted and less remediable than the imperfections of the market. The historians persistently overlook three self-defeating tendencies of government that claims to be armed with the cures for market imperfection. *First,* their remedies are begun too soon. *Second,* they are endemically operated too far. *Third,* they are continued too long. The total effect is that governments cannot be adjusted to the advancing superiorities of the market. Crucially, their measures cannot be withdrawn when the market makes them superfluous.

Government remedies are begun before the market's imperfections have been removed by growing knowledge of its continuing flow of new, competing alternatives. They are applied too widely to where the market has not yet emerged, but could have been foreseen, to where it is expanding. And they are maintained long after they have become superfluous and could be replaced by the new supplies and demands.

Ample illustrations follow in succeeding pages. The government created by democracy has invariably grown too far because it was originated too soon by a simple error in circular reasoning.

Of the four categories of government activities that have deteriorated into over-government the form that most intimately affects everyday life has been given the most benevolent title, "welfare," but has most damaged individual and family life. The virtual destruction of the family, not least among the lower-paid groups in the old industrial regions, is the consequence of the usurpation by the state of the authority of parents.

The fallacious pretext for the welfare state from its beginnings in the late nineteenth century was that desirable services were not being sought by families themselves. This claim is not only historically unfounded. It is rooted in a logical error.

The truth of the origins of welfare in Britain has been surprisingly neglected by English historians. The evidence is demonstrated by 20 authors in two IEA studies: *The Long Debate on Poverty* in 1972, and *Re-privatising Welfare: After the Lost Century* in 1996. The historical evidence shows that by the 1860s most working-class children were at schools paid for by parents with the aid sometimes of the Church or lay charity. By the 1870s some working-class families, especially in the industrial North where wages were higher than in the rural South around London, were beginning to buy their homes with the aid of building societies. By the early 1910s most working-class heads of families were insuring against unemployment, sickness, and ageing. The notion that the working classes of England neglected their families until the state compelled them by law is historical fiction.

The logical error remains a weakness of a century of British economic and social history. The flaw, still repeated in the latest assessments of the welfare state, is that government had to establish the early forms of the welfare state because the people had been unable or unwilling to provide for themselves and their families. Poverty or irresponsibility therefore impelled the state to establish the first "board" schools in 1870, the first compulsory "national" insurance in 1911, the first council houses in 1922, the first compulsory health insurance in 1925, the "National" Health Service in 1948, and other mislabelled "essential" services in the twentieth century.

This neglect of the amply documented history of the common people is the source of the circular reasoning that ironically validated the most conspicuous and persistent growth of over-government. The historical truth is that the precipitate creation of the main (and most minor) forms of state welfare was the very reason why the private forms of welfare, gradually but voluntarily built by the people through "mutual," "friendly" and co-operative societies to the "industrial assurance" of the commercial companies, were in 1946–48 restrained from further expansion. Some were weakened, others expired.

The even more disagreeable political truth is that the state also weakened and finally almost destroyed in Britain an elemental impulse of instinctive

Judaeo-Christian compassion—the charitable giving that, as North American experience indicates, would have grown with rising incomes and general affluence.

A sad sequel is the belated rediscovery in recent months of the "mutual" insurance societies by academics and others who had supported the post-war state policies that almost destroyed them. The recent confession in *The New Statesman* is that "the non-profit 'mutual' and the commercial companies have seemed destined for extinction. But welfare privatisation could yet spectacularly revive them."

This reversal of historical judgement has come 40 years after Beveridge saw the dangerous toy he had innocently given to the politicians. Only five years after his report on social services in 1942 he was moved to warn of the consequences of political irresponsibility in *Voluntary Action.*

The most regrettable political offence, first, in the premature creation, second, the excessive expansion, and, third, the long overdue winding-up of the welfare state is their weakening of working-class family lives. If, when incomes were too low, the state had provided welfare services "free" or at low cost, and promptly withdrawn them with social advance and scientific progress, the British "working classes" would long ago have reached "middle-class" standards.

Few parents would by now be using state schools when and where they have deteriorated. Few working-class families would now be living in the council houses and none in the mugging enclaves of the high-rise tower blocks. Few or none would be allowing ageing parents to wait a year or more for cataract, hip replacement or knee surgery. And almost all would be reaping the advantages of voluntary insurance with mutual or commercial insurers.

The excuse of low-income poverty might have been plausible until the early 1900s. Professor Michael Beenstock has called it evocatively "the Lost Century," based on the analysis by Professor Simon Kuznets: the rising real incomes in the long Industrial Revolution from the late eighteenth to the late nineteenth century could have enabled the "working classes" to pay for the welfare they wanted instead of being tied to the welfare state long after it was outdated. But once tied they are still now being held captive.

The first massive wrong turning, introduced by politicians of the calibre of Lloyd George and Winston Churchill, advised by the academic and later MP William Beveridge, was the introduction in 1911 of compulsory national insurance for working-class heads of families when most were covered, as

Dr. David Green's researches have revealed. This failure to look forward was government "too soon." It dramatises the tendency of politicians to look back rather than forward to the trends or probabilities that would make their measures outdated. The market does not look back. Its critics often blame it for looking forward too far and stimulating "unnecessary" new purchases.

The opposite error of government "too long" is seen in the intention of the 1997 Government to maintain the National Health Service for a further 50 years. This political gesture may charitably be interpreted as continuing assurance that low-income older people can expect free medical care for the rest of their lives. But their children will reject the long waiting and general regulatory flavour of state medical care.

The NHS has persistently failed to raise as much financing as the people would willingly pay for advancing medical care without its long waiting. Research from the 1960s to the 1980s into the methods of financing medical care in the mixed systems of voluntary private and compulsory state insurance in other English-speaking countries and Europe has taught that a state medical system would forever remain chronically "underfunded."

For decades the mixed state and private financing systems have yielded much more "funding" than taxes. They have raised some 8 per cent of national income for medical care in Europe and 10 per cent or more in North America. Since the tax-financed British National Health Service had barely raised 6 per cent, it had limited total national financing to 70–75 per cent of Europe's and 60 per cent of North America's.

By discouraging private insurance the NHS has been the main cause of the "underfunding" of medical care. British governments have in effect prevented the people from spending as much on improving medical care as they would have wished.

The verdict of the historical research is unavoidable. It is the state itself that created the political "necessity" for the welfare state. The more welfare it created by taxation (partly re-christened "social insurance contributions") the more it weakened private financing. The more private welfare it inhibited the more state welfare it had to create.

British government has now so irretrievably "under-funded" the welfare services that it is in self-made crisis: it must abandon the long-promised state welfare and induce the people to return to private financing. The beginning with pensions will have to be followed in medicine, education and elsewhere. The coming generation of wage-earners will not tolerate for its children the third-rate services that failed its parents.

The state created the pretext for its expansion and has now commendably but reluctantly confessed failure. That it describes measures to save the welfare state as "reform" or "modernisation" is more political adroitness of language than historical truth.

The circular reasoning in medical care applies no less to other British state welfare failures. The more "board" schools the state built after 1870, the more private schools closed down. The more the state expanded its old age pension the less people saved themselves and the less they were helped by charitable organisations. The more local government built council housing the fewer private homes for letting or sale were built by private builders.

The welfare state was a political contrivance: an artificial creation of the state, by the state, for the state and its employees. It is an ironic echo of Lincoln's democracy as government of, by, and for "the people."

When its well-concealed but increasing excesses and abuses in central and local government were revealed in recent years, it was after a century of fallacious defence.

The state schools deprived working-class parents of the power to withdraw their children from the worst. The private school parents know that their power to move is the source of their influence on their schools. The power of low-income people to withdraw their children from poor schools, in practice or by intention, was taken from them by the state.

Studies of the inadequacies of state schooling rarely if ever contrast their method of financing with that of the private schools. No further administrative reconstruction by the new Secretary of State for Education, or requiring parents to assist teachers, will improve the standards of the state schools, avoid their wastes of truancy, prevent the physical abuse of teachers, or remove numerous other failings unless he gives parents the power to remove their children.

The superfluous outdated activities of democratic government were continued too long after the 1939–45 War in all four main kinds of state services. The earliest category of "public goods" was wrongly thought necessarily supplied by government. National defence and "law and order" seemed the most obvious but others, not least in local government, were expanded for a century until the 1980s.

What are now called "public utilities" were mostly begun with the rapid growth of industrial towns in the early–mid 1800s. The absence of water and sewage services created anxiety about "public health" that led to action by local government or other "public" authorities. But again the action was continued without systematic inquiries into the necessity for long-continued state control.

The third and fourth groups of welfare and local government services have been discussed above.

These are the services established by government too soon.

Over-Government — Too Far

After enlarging itself too soon, government expands itself too far.

It has become excessive by over-estimating the scope for its rôle. Yet it is being followed by a new wave of official paternalism in its precautions and prohibitions against a range of risks supposedly endangering life. The arguable motives range from the laudable anxiety to prevent the spread of infectious or contagious disease to the political purpose of demonstrating government protection of the innocent populace. Since the 1921 classic study of *Risk, Uncertainty and Profit* by the eminent economist Frank Knight of the University of Chicago, his economist followers have distinguished between costed risk and uncosted uncertainty. Risk is insurable because the probability that it will recur can be calculated from the record of its recurrence. It can be turned into a known cost by insurance, and individuals can judge whether the cost is preferred to the risk. Uncertainty describes the risks that do not occur with sufficient regularity to be insurable.

The uncertainties for which government operates compulsory insurance or outright prohibition by law are generally risks the likelihood of which can be calculated. Dr. Frank Furedi of the University of Kent has compared the risks of a range of possible or probable dangers in diet, road travel, freak weather, and others. The chances are one in very large numbers (Table A).

The efforts of government to discover risks and show anxiety to protect the public can be reassuring. But they can be a rich source of apparently beneficial government—and finally over-government. On the day an official Committee announced a possible risk from eating beef on the bone, the British Secretary of State for Agriculture entered the House of Commons with an official prohibition of its sale. A European Safety Commission has employed 120 researchers into such rare risks as children choking on the small plastic toys enclosed in cereal packets. Britain's Chief Medical Officer of Health has classified unlikely risks:

- less than one in a million—"negligible"
- less than one in 100,000—"minimal"
- less than one in 10,000—"very low"

Table A. Risk and political over-insurance (probability of occurrence)

Possible danger	One in
Struck by lightning	10,000,000
Dying in a plane crash	10,000,000
Beef (CJD)	1,000,000
Falling under a bus	1,000,000
Dying in a railway accident	500,000
Choking on food	250,000
Death from accident at home	26,000
Dying in a football match	25,000
Death from road accident	8,000
Death from influenza	5,000

Source: Frank Furedi, "Obsessed by Safety," *Daily Mail,* 13 December 1997.

The risk from beef was officially "negligible," but democratic government, sensitive to public opinion, judges that it is wiser to show concern for the voter by issuing warnings too soon rather than too late.

The implications are far-reaching. Three stand out. *First,* low risks can plausibly be decided as ripe for insurance because the cost to individuals in taxes is unknown; not surprisingly, if individuals are asked in opinion polling they are likely to approve of everything they think costs them nothing (below, pp. 114–115). But individuals who bear the cost themselves might have preferred to run the small risk and use the money for a different purpose they prefer. The financial "free"-dom of the welfare state has been a cause of much ignorance, uninformed choices, reluctance to provide money for improvement and investment, and waste of resources.

Second, the province of the family has been invaded. The authority of parents has again been usurped and weakened in the control of growing children.

Third, experience of risk and judgement of its cost are part of the everyday process of experience and reflection that teaches humans how to live more safely. This personal process is weakened or destroyed if it is surrendered to the political process. Its loss to individuals in private life has been understood too slowly, but private institutions that provided protection against risk by insurance are gradually being rebuilt. A fundamental reconsideration of the role of risk and its management by individual foresight is long overdue.

In his *Song of The English* Kipling wrote of blood as "the price of Admiralty." The exploitation of risk is part of "the high price of politics."

Over-Government — Too Long

There may once have been plausible ground for the establishment by the state of a desirable service that had spread too slowly among the populace.

Even if it had been thought that this historic excuse for a government initiative had applied to the ostensibly most desirable human service of medical care soon after the Second World War, the subsequent years have by now amply revealed that it was also an historic blunder to have continued it for 50 years.

Economic and scientific advance were soon fundamentally and rapidly changing the conditions of the supply and of the demand for medical care of rising quality and prompt availability that would be far beyond the capacity and resources of a centralised, tax-financed organisation.

The "free" National Health Service established in 1948 can be seen in the light of the subsequent events to have become government activity continued too long. The general rise in real incomes, lagging total state expenditure on medical care, the lengthening queues unknown in any other English-speaking or European country, the continued loss of doctors to the USA and Canada, Australia, New Zealand and elsewhere, improvements in medical science, the growth in private health insurance with early access to medical advice without queueing: all these and more would have produced a much higher quality of medical care in Britain.

The characteristic failure and political fiction of "free" medicine is that for many people with the lowest incomes it has not been available when, where, or how it was wanted. The evidence of history is that it would have been available in all three respects if the government of democracy had allowed it to continue developing as private medicine from its early beginnings.

Yet in 1997, the fiftieth year of the largely unchanged NHS, it was again reconstructed on the same assumptions of 1947—that all it required was goodwill from doctors, nurses and other staff, and patients would readily accept that all would be well.

The three fundamental fallacies in the faith in the National Health Service were and are still ignored. Not least was the claim, repeated to this day, that it was "the envy of the world" despite the continuing decision of all comparable countries to reject it.

The further false claim that it offered the highest quality of medical care in the world was obscured by the widespread experience that it was ironically not available at all when it was most wanted. The plausible emphasis on priority for "acute" cases did not obscure the anxieties, deterioration of symptoms, or the burden heaped on the families of the chronically sick.

Not least the advantage of closer and prompter attention to the culturally advanced higher-income patients who could persuasively argue for earlier treatment than the culturally weaker was not acknowledged by the suppliers—the doctors.

The fundamental economic transformation, largely ignored by the sociologists, was that the National Health Service had replaced a developing buyers' market for medical attention by a sellers' market. That was clear to the economic mind that studied the contrasting bargaining power of buyers and sellers in state medicine and open markets. But neither was it generally acknowledged by the political scientists or politicians who saw only a service that required a periodic infusion of more tax funds. The ailing tax-financing system was made incurable at its core by the lack of guidance from the crucial prices of scarce medical resources that required scrupulous care to guard against over-use.

The plausible but flawed complaint of "under-funded" obscured the true cause of the inadequacies of the NHS. That truth soon became obvious when in 1968 I was asked by the British Medical Association to join a committee of 10 medical men (with one other "patient," later a Chancellor of the Exchequer) to recommend fundamental reform in the funding of medical care. Nowhere else in the world, except the USSR and other communist countries, were the people largely limited to state financing of medical care.

But in Britain the internal "barnacles"—the political, professional and trade union interests—tenaciously resisted reform. Influence on policy lay largely with the doctors as the respected or feared experts whose judgement could hardly be challenged by amateur patients. Economic advance and scientific progress will before long change bargaining power back to the buyers' markets that were developing before the NHS.

The 1997–98 switches of tax funds from some early forms of internal medical markets, which had introduced invaluable pricing, to reduce waiting-lists will not end the periodic breakdowns. The crucial reform is the empowerment of the consumer to escape when dissatisfied. This power will be created by increasing private insurance, emulating his great-grandfather of the 1900s.

British governments have also persistently refused to recognise the embarrassing truth that the quality of state schooling, with exceptions, will not be raised except by empowering parents to escape from schools that ill-educate their children. In the past 50 years governments have fabricated a string of administrative reconstructions that were presented as the final solution but are little more than patching or re-patching of previous government failures.

Here again the lower-income parents often lack the cultural power to argue their case with school authorities. Their grown-up children with higher living standards will in their turn hardly abandon their young to the failing state schools.

Ironically, the superior teaching of the schools that recognise "parent power" and the ultimate parents' sanction of withdrawing their children, long condemned as "privilege," is having to be accepted by the long line of supporters of state education. Government is finally inviting the expertise and experience of competing private schools, with the implicit threat of sanctions on recalcitrant state schools held in reserve.

Nor will the families with rising incomes gladly move into the Council houses left to them by the million and more of their parents who bought them on good terms in the 1980s. They will hardly want to live in the Council housing that five million of their parents acquired as tenants even on favourable rents in the past decades. The loss in the capital value of real estate owned by the taxpayers, with large bills for repairs or redevelopment as the costly alternative, will be very large.

It has taken most of the post-war experience to teach the human cost of government that has continued too long. From its earliest years the Institute's studies revealed the coming inability of government to continue its excesses, frictions and tensions. A fundamental limitation on government was its inability to raise the required funds from willing taxpayers. Previous politicians in power sensed earlier doubts, but the new 1997 Government has articulated the fundamental truth that, even if it wished to continue the swelling volume of government activities, the populace were clearly in no mood to pay the mounting bills.

Two political statements show the new readiness of government to accept the change in taxpayer attitudes and powers. The 1997 Prime Minister warned that taxpayers were asking "fundamental questions about how much we [governments] spend and how we spend it." And the Minister of Welfare Reform, who has learned from the errors of urging higher spending on people "in need," has been the most ready of his Ministerial colleagues to warn that the prospect of ever-rising government expenditures has at last ended. Mr. Frank Field has had to use graphic language directed at the politicians still hopeful of large and even increasing government: "We are ceasing to live in a society where taxpayers let us put our hands into their pockets and take out more money."

The political danger is that his colleagues are advised by academics and others who had urged the high-spending, high-taxing policies over the decades and may too easily relapse into error when the predictable opposition to high-taxing is seen as the signal to low-spending (and low-voting or no-voting).

The task is now to see not only how far normally law-abiding citizens can escape from what they consider unjustified taxation in an economy with over-government. The latest technical devices to detect offenders—roadblocks for interrogation of possible commercial tax-evaders and the "informer" telephone-lines—could discover some tax-revenue but lose even more by further alienating potential taxpayers.

Government is increasingly caught in the dilemma of democracy. The fundamental conclusion from the evidence examined in this Paper is repeatedly that it is becoming too late for government to withdraw from over-government. Two developments may follow.

It is becoming increasingly urgent to discover new political men, and women, who see the dangers for democracy sufficiently to embrace economic advance and scientific progress in resisting the barnacles. But it may not be sufficient to withdraw over-government to its minimum. To prevent a return to over-government it would be necessary to replace over-government by under-government in which the risks of economic progress from which individuals can learn to avoid or bear are returned from government to the people.

The unresolved dilemma of over-spending and under-taxing has increasingly misled the state for a century. Its fiscal powers no longer suffice, and its moral writ no longer runs, to make "society" pay for over-government.

Over-Government by Barnacle

Trade unions, professional associations, industrial organisations, special interests of all kinds, from artistic to environmental, not only demand increased government expenditure but also oppose reductions that would limit their activities, power, influence, and incomes.

They deploy the most persuasive agents in the most persuasive argument that cannot easily be disproved. Their universal claim is that the activities they favour are "underfunded": that they could do good with more money.

This repeated formula is an apparent evident truth that throws no light on the distribution by government of the innumerable and unlimited calls on its tax revenues. There are two flaws in the plausible plea from the "under-funded." They offer mostly unsupportable claims that their activities are "vital" for the eventual good of the people—from the spiritual uplift of grand opera sung by wealthy tenors or sopranos, through the preservation of hedgerows by subsidised farmers, to the early rescue from global warming by scientists who could do more good improving the ventilation of working-class homes. And they universally fail to pass the essential test of more "funding": that it will do more good than in any alternative activity.

The task of government, *which it cannot perform because it deprives itself of the information,* is to decide the good that its allocation of funds will do in all alternative uses. Every human activity can do more good with more resources. Extra expenditure on the arts will produce more or better opera singers. But that is not the important decision for government. It has to demonstrate that the money would not do more good elsewhere. It must therefore show that additional ("marginal") utility in all possible uses has been equalised so that no more "good" can in total be done by transferring resources from where they do less good to where they can do more.

The result is that all the interests are unconsciously ganging up to force government to continue old activities when they could increasingly be financed by individuals—with the additional advantage that they would know how much satisfaction they received.

The financial acid test of most "public" services is whether the people for whom they are supposedly intended would pay for them. Let government and subsidised "public" services be judged not by politicians and lobbyists but by the people for whom they are intended. Let the Royal Opera House, Covent Garden, pay for itself by charging for all seats enough to pay its costs. There would then be less extravagant scenic stages, lower salaries for millionaire international tenors and sopranos, but more charitable prestige subsidies from the banks and insurance companies, and more provincial companies like Kent Opera and Opera Brava for middling-income and middle-brow enthusiasts.

There would also be lower subsidies for farmers on the North Wales hillsides, more young scientists doing more good for the century in which they live than for the next, lower Council subsidies for affluent golfers, and above all lower taxes for alienated taxpayers.

Over-Government by Stealth

Of all the expedients employed by the democratic state to require or justify over-expansion of government, the exaggeration of risk (Chapter 2) has been used to inflate the use of national "social" insurance.

The system has now degenerated into an openly confessed deceit as a substitute form of taxation. But even the promise of higher-rate insurance benefits for the widening range of risks to keep pace with inflation has now been accepted by government as inadequate and impracticable.

The state introduced the system unnecessarily in 1911 to cover employed men when most had long been covered by competing private insurers offering a much wider range of benefits to suit individual and family circumstances.

A subtle justification for "social" insurance is still used, among others by Lord Longford, who worked for Beveridge on his 1942 Report, to justify the continued use of social insurance nearly 50 years after it was introduced. Even in the late 1940s it was urged long after the conditions that may plausibly have justified it, as a temporary expedient to provide for continuing poverty, had passed.

"Social" insurance is still a main financial bastion of the welfare state. But its ingenious justification by Winston Churchill—that "the magic of averages" had come to "succour the millions"—does not excuse its continuance into the twenty-first century. Homer nodded. This is the totalitarian remedy of equalising conditions for unequal people. In time it has become apparent that, as Churchill could have said of social insurance when he was Prime Minister in 1951, "The fiction of averages has come to plague the untypical individual."

In a growing economy no individuals are widely or permanently "average." For people in industries differing in local or international markets, or seasonal employment, or in areas with growing or declining industries, the state offered a uniform benefit that was inadequate for some families and unnecessarily costly for others. Social insurance was needlessly uniform. Post-war governments knew, not least, that by the late 1940s and into the 1950s the trend was for millions of employees to be covered by employers' occupational pension schemes. But once the state has introduced new approaches or institutions it cannot easily adapt them to new circumstances. Even if it sees its errors, it is entrapped by the plausible plea that they be allowed time to prove themselves: a plausible excuse for continuing state action when it is outdated. Lord Longford may not have seen reason in 1998 for the state to remove itself from welfare activities that the people could perform better for themselves. Lord Beveridge quickly saw the dangers 50 years earlier in 1947 when he repented by writing *Voluntary Action.*

Over-Government by Alibi

In the early years of the Institute doubts were raised about post-war opinion polling that claimed widespread readiness of the people—often around 80 per cent—to pay higher taxes for more expenditure on state welfare.

By 1963 it was evident that the polls were misleading everyone—not only editors of newspapers but, surprisingly, university academics and politicians on all sides encouraged to win popularity by higher spending.

Yet the fallacy should also have been clear. When pricing was introduced into the IEA field surveys the usual relationship between price and demand was soon revealed: the demand for state welfare rose with lower tax-costs and fell with higher tax-costs.

Over-Government by Stampede

Democratic government has been inflated by political over-sensitivity to exaggeration, rumour and confusion on the risks of environmental damage.

The fallacies in the extravaganzas of the environmentalists are mainly five: exaggeration of the evidence, questionable deduction, the confusion between inherent risks (in food or medicines) and amounts or doses, neglect of the costs of prevention, and the allocation of surmised benefit over the unknown generations.

The environmental argument for emergency measures in the twentieth century is as fallacious as Thomas Malthus's population scare of the early nineteenth. It has similar elements of influence on public anxiety: unsubstantiated but plausible warnings of the risk of severe danger to mankind.

Malthus forewarned that the population would grow much faster by geometrical progression, as families more than reproduced themselves, than would the world means of subsistence to feed them which increased only by arithmetical progression in agricultural improvement.

For decades the fear of over-population persisted. But Malthus had underestimated the rate of nineteenth-century technological innovation that raised the production of food by much more than the increase in population. Living standards rose faster than in any previous century. The present-day environmentalist overlooks the power of probable but unexpected scientific advance to discover new preventives or treatments for their worst fears without equipping government with more powers that it will not relax when they are found superfluous.

The environmentalists have learned nothing from British history, except the fallacy that government is the infallible instrument of human benevolence. And it repeats the facile failure of other petitioners for the taxpayer's penny or pound—to show the opportunity cost of the alternatives sacrificed.

Malthus's 1798 warning in his *Essay on the Principle of Population* may have restrained the size of families and possibly increased investment in agricultural machinery for food production. The twentieth-century environmentalists may likewise induce caution in the preservation of animal and vegetable life. But the most likely expectation is that since their crusade rests on the same over-estimation of risk in all other walks of life, it will add to over-government.

This is a summary review of the (so far) seven main sources of the over-government that would have to be disciplined and abandoned if democracy is to remain the political foundation of Western civilisation.

The opposite tendency is the likelihood that the escapes from over-government analysed by economists will increase in the twenty-first century. The future of democracy will depend on its ability to reduce its over-government to the size, extent, weight or mass acceptable to the people as shown by their readiness to pay for state services.

The more and wider the escapes (reviewed below, Chapter 3), the smaller acceptable government will have to shrink. The most acceptable size would be that which ran the risks of under-government. Optimum government is better small because it is politically easier to enlarge rather than to reduce too much. And, as the market liberates exchange, it increasingly empowers the people to order withdrawal. Thomas Hobbes's "state of nature" without "sovereignty" was a seventeenth-century nightmare. Democratic market supremacy over rogue government is a twenty-first-century dawn.

The escapes are emerging from accelerating changes in supply and demand for goods and services that are forming new and more accessible markets outside the control of government for all peoples in all countries.

CHAPTER 3

The Escapes from Over-Government

Escape by Science

The ability of democracy to create over-government was strongest when the services of government, good, bad or indifferent, were difficult or costly to escape. Defence by the state against external enemies was always inefficient but costly or impracticable to replace by local private defence when the tools of war became complex.

The two kinds of escapes from government services are now growing fast. They are the fundamental universal defences of liberty in economic life—unrestricted access to changing supply and demand. They operate everywhere, seen or unseen. Governments cannot finally suppress them, as the communist régimes of Europe and Asia discovered. But they are most effective and powerful wherever individuals or groups can arrange exchanges with each other in open markets.

The main engine of rapidly advancing sophisticated supply is the discovery of new, simpler, cheaper devices of production and distribution of goods and services tailored to individual circumstances and preferences.

A fundamental deficiency of state services, in the advance of the affluence that is enabling more to escape from over-government, is the cultural difference that paradoxically disadvantages the lower-income families to the benefit of the higher-incomes.

The criticism by Fabian writers of the nineteenth-century markets for goods and services of all kinds, that they favoured the monied people, was basically valid. The access to the best products was determined or influenced by the possession of purchasing power. The retort of the political scientist Harold Laski to his liberal market colleagues at the 1930s London School of Economics that "The poor had equal access to the Ritz [Hotel] with the rich" was then true. Yet it stopped short at the ultimate truth that the solution was not to establish a socialised Ritz and supply it universally "free."

The truth is that government replaces the old inequality of financial power in markets by unequal cultural power in the realm of the state that is even more difficult to eradicate.

The recent proposal of the 1997 Government to remove the disabilities of the "Socially Excluded" by easing access to state services would replace them by the deeper-rooted cultural inequality in access to state education, medical care and many more. The differences of family origin, accent, education, occupational connections and the ability to make a case with the controllers of state services are more difficult to remove than financial differences, especially if it is done by lowering taxes and enabling the lower-income people to exercise the same market power of withdrawing their purchasing power if dissatisfied, as higher-income people have long been able to do.

Yet scientific advance is creating easier escape from standardised state services by producing wider ranges of goods and services more easily adapted to individual differences. This sensitivity to individual circumstance and preference would then increasingly spread to the "public" supply of education, medical care and other services as it has long spread in private competitively-supplied food and clothing, home furnishings and homes, domestic amenities and leisure pursuits that have raised working-class living standards.

Escape by Affluence

Rising incomes will enable many families that have passively or unthinkingly accepted the nearest school or the usual family doctor to become better able to pay for services suited to their varying requirements and more demanding in their expectations of school results and medical performance.

Administrative reconstruction of state school teaching and state medicine will not be able to keep pace with the dissatisfaction of parents and patients. The escape from the state will accelerate in the twenty-first century.

The trend will be especially rapid where children are reared in families that remain cohesive rather than where they succumb to passing fashions in looser lifestyles. The rate of increase in family incomes will produce advances in the home and domestic lifestyles of children that will make families more internally supportive.

Moreover, children who have done well in life will hardly allow their parents or more distant elderly relatives to wait endlessly for cataract, hip or knee surgery or endure inferior conditions when sick. They will wish to assist siblings and other relatives with private education. Internal family assistance will extend from unusually generous offerings on birthdays, marriages and seasonal occasions to more formal assistance with allowances to top up low earnings. The family will survive and prosper as the welfare state is replaced by competitive private services.

Internal private redistribution of income was more common in middling-income families than it became after the state nationalised "giving." Politicised collective charity through taxation has diminished not only the charitable instinct to succour the needy but also weakened the financial self-help of the family. Charity for the remaining needy and self-help within the family will spread among the lower-income groups in the coming decades.

Of the vast array of "public" services developed in the twentieth century few are now necessarily supplied by government. Some of the so-called "public" goods, few of the "public" utilities, very few "social" (welfare) services, and even fewer local services have to be produced, managed, sold or financed by the political process of democracy.

Around half of all the services, functions, financing and other activities now owned, controlled, regulated or financed by government could be supplied by a widening variety of private institutions. They would be individuals, firms, mutual associations, voluntary organisations, corporations and societies, charities and benevolent groups, and other spontaneous activities that would emerge if the state withdrew from its over-grown domain.

The difficulty has been that individuals and families could not build organisations—smaller, more varied, more personalised—that would create, for themselves or for sale to others, "bespoke" rather than "off-the-peg" goods and services. And the difference, even as recently as only 25 years ago, is that most of the services supplied by the state no longer have to be bought from government and paid for by taxes.

It is now possible to escape from most of them, and so halve the reach and writ of government. Taxation could be reduced from more than 40 per cent to less than 20 per cent of personal and private earnings.

The reasons are not far to seek. They are all around us in our daily lives. We are aware of some of the most recent, but strangely oblivious of the most familiar and obvious.

The upward trend in earnings and other incomes will enable more people to buy goods and services of better individual quality than the state can ever provide.

The "public" goods of law and order can in part be supplied by competing private suppliers. Not the least important, the "public service" once regarded as essential, is perhaps the least expected. The British are being protected from loss of possessions and personal assault by private police forces.

And when the offenders are caught they are increasingly prevented from doing harm by being housed in private prisons and other places of detention.

This movement from "public" (political) to private has been broadly the trend in our life-times since and before the last war. But the upward trend in quality will now be much faster.

Escape to Personal Services

The growth in recent years of the number of people who do not work on the premises of their employers is in large part the result of technologies that maintain communications by computers. It is also, if less clearly, a subconscious intention to escape, or at least to minimise, taxes on earnings, not least by reducing taxable work.

Income earned from services such as consultancy or advisory yields economies of scale in selling to several purchasers who pay by fees rather than salaries. Work that can be done at home rather than at the employer's premises replaces physical transport by wired communications.

The new technical marvels have not yet reached most people. But their children are learning them at school—even, but more slowly, at state schools. And parents will want to learn faster to maintain family communications (below, pp. 135–40).

Escape to the Parallel Economy

Over-government is overlooking the opportunity cost of making taxes more difficult to reject by avoidance or evasion. The more successful the measures to maximise tax collection the lower the net earnings in the "parallel" economy of barter or other methods of escaping taxes as well as in the "official" economies. But the lower therefore will be the production of goods and services, the more poverty will remain, and the longer inequalities will persist.

The escape from over-taxation has produced a forest of labels to describe the motivations or intentions of the escapers.

In principle, the three aspects of tax rejection—legal, economic and moral—remain in the wide range of labels from "black," to denote crude defiance of the law, through a string of labels to embrace mixtures of motives—informal, unrecorded, shadow, and others—to the so far little-used but most appropriate term, "parallel" economy. It emerged in discussion with a Swiss economist on the calculations in the *World Competitiveness Report* and the extent of production outside the "official" statistics in the reports from the OECD and other international organisations. "Parallel" seemed the most convenient as a neutral term to describe the "unofficial" production of national product and income. The total of "official" and "unofficial" ("parallel") economies would then measure the full range of productive activities and complete the calculations of total production or incomes. The term "parallel" also avoided moral judgement of the responsibility for tax rejection, whether government or people, the taxers or the taxed.

For neutral observers analysing the economics of productive life "parallel" avoids the allotment of moral responsibility between the government tax creators, for over-estimating the readiness of taxpayers to share their earnings with government, and the individual tax rejectors, for declining justifiable taxes. Economic interest lies in the total production of the goods and services that raise standards of living, diminish poverty, reduce inequality and have other beneficial effects, whatever the motives of the producers.

To work with taxpayers who like paying taxes must be the understandable hope of every new politician who enters Parliament to win appreciation and power from the electors.

The accord between the policy-makers, who decide their electors' payment by taxes, and the taxpayers, who cannot assess the services of monopoly government, can be judged only by the readiness to pay taxes without question. Government services, taxpayers should think, are good value; "we" elected "them"; so we should pay for what they give us without complaint.

The historic democratic compact, the "social contract" between government and people, was based on the voluntary exchange of government respect for the people and the people's trust in government. It reflected the acceptance of government decisions and the taxes it levied as necessary for good order. Historians have yet to study the changing relationships of mutual respect between government and people in Britain. The past century of growing over-government, and its implied disrespect for the capacity of the people to learn from liberty, to make decisions, to assess the unavoidable uncertainties in human life, to treat adults as children who have failed to grow with experience, have created disillusion with "democracy," mistrust of politicians as a self-appointed superior breed, and fomented reluctance to pay their taxes.

Neither government nor taxpayer has to sell to or buy from the other most of the services they exchange. For some taxpayers mutual respect has been increasingly replaced by doubt and resentment. The evidence is the emergence of numerous varied trading devices that facilitate the (legal) avoidance or (illegal) evasion of taxes.

The latest development in government methods to detect tax avoiders or evaders—road-blocks to question suspected drivers and "informer" telephone lines—may garner modest amounts in taxes from small traders and occasional evening or week-end earners. But they raise anxious questions about the relationship of trust between government and people and the role of politicians as servants or masters of the people.

In the relationship of buyers and sellers of services over-government has bred indifferent politicised suppliers and reluctant consumer-buyers. The transformation from mutual respect to mutual suspicion, the estrangement between government and people is the natural reaction of consumers faced with a monopoly—"public" or private—that betrays its lack of confidence in itself by denying escape to competitors. The Chancellor of the Exchequer in his budgets of June 1997, November 1997 and March 1998 sounded new notes of aggrieved unpaid creditor rather than as supplier of services on good terms with his satisfied prompt-paying customers.

The manageable "black" market of the inter-war and early post-war years has been replaced by widening varieties of tax-rejection that defy the easy descriptions of politicians and government officials. It is no longer sufficient to imply a deep moral gulf between virtuous tax-creators and venal tax-resisters. The gulf was long called "black" to emphasise the contrast or conflict between government and people. The "informal" or "shadow" economies implied a lower degree of conflict or contrast. The "underground" better conveyed the French spirit of war-time resistance to oppression.

The more recent term that avoids moral judgement between government and people—the "parallel" economy—requires a more searching analysis of the necessity and defects of taxes.

A straw poll has been attempted by recent governments to gauge the general sentiment on "public services" based on the series of Charter undertakings to supply high quality with penalties for failure. In 1997 it requested, from the real "public" of the people, nominations of "Charter Mark" awards by government to organisations judged to have given good service. The Cabinet Office or its nominees received 29,000 nominations for 10,000 local services. The 1998 Charter Mark scheme circulated examples of services that might qualify for nomination:

schools	local library
the police	leisure centre
ambulance services	refuse collection
fire services	housing
doctors	benefits agencies

dentists	job centres
hospitals	tax offices
clinics	others

Nominations could be for (one or more) awards of a Charter Mark in six categories of satisfaction:

- "excellent" service
- complaints promptly settled
- staff helpful and polite
- "efficient" service
- service beyond expectations
- other reasons

Nominations could be submitted by post, telephone, on the Internet by E-mail or to the web-site. Evidently more of the public know the Internet than is commonly supposed.

Whatever the substantive value of the Charters, which must be questioned since they list aspects of services long assumed to be the very purpose of "public" services, or the authenticity of the nominations, it is clearly difficult for government to know how far general taxpayers or specific beneficiaries are content. There are no alternative services with which taxpayers can compare them. Nor is there return of taxes to dissatisfied recipients. The value of this effort to gauge public satisfaction must remain unestablished, especially in terms of its costs, the small response and the obscurity of the nominations.

The satisfaction of taxpayers must ultimately remain to be measured by their willingness to pay taxes for government services. Neither governments nor academic students of the fiscal system know how many pay their taxes gladly, why some pay little or nothing, or their reasons. The parallel economy, which produces no taxes on a wide and accelerating range of productive activity, is surprisingly little studied by political scientists and sociologists, or even by economists who judge the production and distribution of national income without the large part that is unrecorded or under-assessed in official government statistics. It is not surprising that so far little is known about its causes and extent.

Three substantial reports on world economic trends have offered information on varying aspects of the parallel economy. The renowned *World Competitiveness Report*, 1995, an absorbing study directed by Professor Stéphane Garelli of the University of Lausanne, was primarily concerned with the elements of economic activity that strengthened or weakened comparative national economic dynamism. A cautious reference to the reluctance to pay taxes may be inferred from his observation that, despite the growth of global competitiveness, national citizens may be "keen to decide upon environmental, social or medical protection . . . [or] to subsidise culture or agriculture . . . through taxes." He thought they "may have preferred to run massive public debt . . . ," the alternative to taxation that had doubled in Europe and the USA in the dozen years to 1995. This massive rise could reveal that it was politically easier to levy taxes on the taxpayers of the next generation, who cannot vote against them, than on their living parents, who know the present pain of reduced incomes after taxes.

Two further world reviews were more explicit on the extent of the less legal forms of tax rejection. The *1996 Index of Economic Freedom* from the Heritage Foundation of Washington, D.C., defined "black markets" as explicitly outlawed by government and graded their rejected taxes. They are shown (Table B) correlated with the taxation of broadly similar countries. The sources for the tax gradings were recent reports from the World Bank, *The Economist* Intelligence Unit and the accountants Price Waterhouse.

The gradings for "black market" were also assessed as components of illegal activity: the extent of smuggling; how far technical appliances (videocassette recorders) were sold by "black"-market traders as evidence of prices raised substantially by tariffs; or workers in illegal activities, as evidence of over-regulation.

These largely outlawed activities exclude the productive economic life of the wider parallel economies which comprise tax rejection as a whole, whatever the inducements or motives. Their incomes may include cash payments—"tips" and others, rents from tenants, self-employee profits, underestimated or under-stated consultancy "fees," barter between individuals or firms, and others.

The total parallel economy is probably much larger than the "outlawed" activities in many countries, especially perhaps in Sweden, Italy, Spain and others.

Illegal "black markets" as identified in the Heritage Reports are created by government laws and regulations. If the parallel economies are substantially larger than these estimates of around 5 per cent for "illegal" tax evasion (for advanced countries unofficial guesses rise to 25 and 30 per cent of GDP—below), governments in many Western democracies have estranged large segments of their normally law-abiding populace. Some light on the causes of their reluctant tax rejection has been shed by further researches (below).

Table B. Taxation and "black" markets, 1996 (as percentage of GDP)

Country	Taxation (grade)	Black markets (grade)
New Zealand	3.5	1
France	4.0	1
Australia	4.0	2
USA	4.0	1
Canada	4.0	1
UK	4.5	1
Austria	4.5	1
Sweden	4.5	1
Netherlands	4.5	1
Japan	4.5	1
Germany	5.0	1
Italy	5.0	1
Spain	5.0	3

Tax grading:	*score 3*—top income tax rate 35 per cent or less
	average taxes below 15 per cent
	score 4—top income tax rate 36–65 per cent
	average taxes 15–20 per cent
	score 5—top income tax rate over 50 per cent
	average income taxes 20–25 per cent
Black market grading:	*score 1*—"very low level"
	score 2—"low level"
	score 3—"moderate level"

Source: *1996 Index of Economic Freedom,* Heritage Foundation, Washington, D.C.

The third world report, for 1997, was prepared for the Fraser Institute of Vancouver and 47 institutes world-wide by Professors James Gwartney of Florida State University and Robert Lawson of Capital University. It intends to examine these further aspects of tax rejection in future Reports.

Higher estimates are offered in the annual *Economist* predictions in its *The World Economy in 1998,* described as "Black Economies" (Table C).

The *Economist* material emboldened its Editor, Dudley Fishburn, to pronounce: ". . . every country's unofficial black economy will [in 1998] do better than its government statistics will show." Its reasons for the "black" economies are listed as high taxes, onerous labour market regulations, red tape that induces "scorn of officialdom," social insurance, sales taxes, cash pay to employees ("often illegal immigrants"), and "paper work" registering a new business. The "shadow" economy was a "healthy response to excessive government interference," but in 1998 tax-leviers would "crack down harder," which would raise the costs of "legitimate" business. The better solution would be to attack excessive regulation and high taxes, otherwise revenue would dwindle.

The latest evidence has come belatedly from the European Commission in its report, *Communication on Undeclared Work* (extracts published in *The European*). The EU document is far from as informative as it could have been but it provokes searching questions and inferences. Its estimates are shown in Table D.

Table C. Black economies in main countries (per cent of GDP)

Switzerland	6
Japan	9
USA	9
Britain	12
Germany	15
France	15
Sweden	18
Spain	23
Italy	24

Source: The Economist: *The World Economy in 1998.*

Table D. The "shadow" labour market in Europe, per cent of GDP (approximations within wide margins)

Greece	35
Italy	26
Spain	23
Belgium	22
Germany	14
France	14
Netherlands	14
Britain	12
Ireland	10
Denmark	8
Austria	8
Sweden	8
Finland	5

Source: European Commission, *Communication on Undeclared Work,* reported in *The European,* 6–12 April 1998.

The EU report is informative on the numerous devices, some ingenious, agreed between employers and employees, to make and accept payment in cash. Its general conclusion, predictable from an international association of governments, is that the solution is "[government] intervention oriented towards punishment." The EU has yet to accept that stricter government enforcement may produce less rather than more tax revenue.

The European output that escapes the tax net is estimated to be produced by 10 to 18 million officially "unemployed," from the high-paid to the low-paid, many of whom may also work as well as claim social benefits.

The European's headings to its review may seem overdramatic: "Millions are moonlighting to make ends meet" and "Going underground is a worker's last resort." Yet the mounting evidence of widespread alienation from democratic government seems incontrovertible. The European Union's "official" total of 18 million unemployed in Europe is almost certainly much too high; 11–12 million would be nearer the true estimate.

What remain to be identified are the diverse causes of the disaffection. Here the most refined researches and analyses have come from Friedrich Schneider, Professor of Economics at the Johannes Kepler University in Austria. His work was discussed at conferences of the European Public Choice Society in the 1980s. British economic policies in the 1970s and earlier had been producing evidence of resentment and resistance to intrusive high taxes. Clearly a fundamental reconsideration of the economic, legal and moral aspects of what seemed a growing part of economic life had become long overdue.

As with many other neglected subjects the IEA was first in the field with *Tax Avoision* in 1979 (above, Introduction), a hybrid title for the hybrid development in fiscal affairs, assembled shortly after a further IEA field survey in 1978 based on prices that cast continuing doubt on the conventional priceless opinion polling.

Professor Schneider had written in a 1980s issue of *Economic Affairs* a general review of the extent of the "shadow" economy. In the September 1997 issue he analysed a more detailed study of 18 countries from the 1960s to 1995, including 11 of the 17 in the OECD. His findings for the "shadow" economy from various dates in the 1960s, 1980 and 1990, with my imagined projections for 2000 and 2010, are shown in Table E.

Professor Schneider's "demand for currency" method of measuring the "shadow" economy is based on the proposition that, because cash transactions are easier to conceal than payments by cheques, credit cards, and other records, the larger the amount of currency in circulation, the larger the probable "shadow" economy.

Table E. The "shadow" economies, 1960s–1995 (measured by the demand-for-currency method)

Country	First date	1980	1990	2000	2010
Austria	0.4 (1960)	3.1	5.3	7	10
Belgium	7.8 (1965)	15.4	19.6	21	25
Canada	6.5 (1975)	10.7	13.5	17	21
Denmark	4.3 (1960)	8.6	11.2	15	20
Germany	2.1 (1960)	10.8	11.8	15	20
France	3.9 (1970)	6.9	9.4	12	25
Italy	8.4 (1965)	16.7	23.4	28	36
Netherlands	4.8 (1970)	9.1	13.9	19	25
Norway	9.5 (1960)	10.6	15.3	20	30
Spain	18.0 (1978)	21.0	21.0	32	40
Sweden	1.7 (1960)	——	12.2	15	20
Switzerland	1.2 (1960)	6.5	9.9	12	17
UK	2.0 (1970)	8.4	10.2	14	19
USA	3.4 (1960)	5.0	6.9	8	12

Source: Friedrich Schneider, "The Shadow Economies of Western Europe," *Economic Affairs*, Vol. 17, No. 3, September 1997.

The "currency-demand" approach is the most widely used method of estimating the "shadow" or parallel economy but omits some forms of tax rejection. Cash is not required for the growing device of barter (pp. 131–33). Objectionable regulations weaken the sense of obligation or exacerbate defiance in paying taxes. Cash in American dollars is virtually an international currency held by people in other countries. The frequency with which currencies are used (the velocity of circulation) probably varies even more in the full parallel economies than in the official economies. The size of parallel economics in the years before the first of these estimates is not known. The estimates are calculated on the generous assumption that there was no tax rejection in the preceding years, so the estimates for all countries are probably far too low.

In spite of these unavoidable limitations the estimates indicate the widespread increase in the shadow economies over recent decades. And the omissions (cash, barter, and so on) make the full parallel economies possibly much larger than the other "unofficial" economies shown in the Tables.

To improve the estimates derived from the limited "currency-demand" method, Professor Schneider persisted with further refinements, incorporating the researches of other economists, of the statistics available since 1965 for his country, Austria. Moreover, they indicated the likely main causes of the increases over 30 years, which is a rare finding in the researches into the causes of payment and non-payment of taxes.

These causes are undoubtedly adaptable to other countries in Europe. It remains for us in Britain to attempt similar calculations and establish more accurate estimates than existing government statistics or guesses.

Four main causes were detected in the more precise statistics for Austria: *first,* the weight of direct taxes, *second,* the weight of indirect taxes; *third,* the complexity of all taxes; and *fourth,* the intensity of detailed government regulation—of industry and private lives. The estimated total shadow economy in each decade from 1965 to 1995 and the four causes are shown in Table F.

The movement in the figures over the 30 years 1965 to 1995 could be repeated for Britain to indicate the reforms urgently required to reduce the British shadow economy. They are: lower direct taxes, lower indirect taxes, simpler taxes, and more comprehensible regulation of industry.

The figures yield intriguing results. The effect of the direct taxes, which were the most potent of the four causes throughout the 30 years, has fallen from the mid-1960s, when it accounted for 51.2 per cent of the shadow economy, to 28.7 per cent in 1995, and was then almost overtaken by the intensity of excessive regulation, 26.0 per cent.

At a time when the British Government is concerned about the loss of tax revenue there is here unique crucial guidance in fiscal and general financial policies.

The apparent influence of indirect taxes in Austria doubled from 1965 to 1995 to account for a quarter of the shadow economy. This trend could be traced in Britain to reveal the responsibility, if any, of VAT or other indirect taxes for the growing parallel economy.

Table F. Growth in the shadow economy in Austria: The four causes of growth, 1965–1995

Year	Total shadow economy % of GDP	Direct taxes % of causation	Indirect taxes % of causation	Complexity of taxes % of causation	Intensity of regulation % of causation
1965	1.16	51.2	12.1	25.9	9.8
1975	1.73	50.9	15.9	23.4	9.8
1985	4.16	44.0	25.2	15.2	15.6
1995	7.20	28.7	26.6	18.7	26.0

Source: Schneider, *op. cit.*

The Austrian tax system seems to have been simplified since 1965, when its complexity apparently explained 25.9 per cent of the shadow economy, and fell to 18.7 per cent in 1995. There is undoubtedly room for simplification of taxes in Britain.

Yet the most striking change in Austria has been the trebling in the intensity of regulation of industry and economic life generally, which increased its responsibility for the shadow economy from a tenth in 1965 (9.8 per cent) to more than a quarter (26.0 per cent) in 1995. This is another warning to Britain about a main culprit in its expanding parallel economy. The growth of almost mercantilist detail (pp. 143–44) in its restrictive regulations of industrial and private life is a clear case for close examination.

Professor Schneider's work shows the degree of refinement in searching for the radical causes of what is becoming instinctive tax rejection. It should be applied in Britain before the Government can assess the full extent and probable causes of the shadow and parallel economies. This task is an essential preliminary to the fundamental reconsideration of British taxes and regulations that the Government seems to be attempting in adjusting the welfare state to the twenty-first century.

The remaining doubt would then be whether the growing disinclination to pay taxes would resist the obstruction of the required reforms. Government may have to accept that British taxpayers will not tolerate the taxes and regulations of past government to deal with painful adjustments to economic change or to satisfy the chorus of "under-funding" from vested interests.

Methods of estimating parallel economies will undoubtedly advance over time. The inter-actions between the "official" and "unofficial" economies are emphasised by Professor Schneider as an early task of research. Lower taxes in Austria in the late 1980s, which might have been expected to reduce tax rejection ("avoision"), were followed by increased rejection. Either taxes were not reduced sufficiently to satisfy taxpayers or the increasing habit of rejecting taxes has been fortified by the new technical and financial methods of escaping from them.

It may be concluded that it is too late in Austria, and in Britain, to solve the democratic dilemma, the choice between reducing over-government despite the widespread displeasure of beneficiaries, or maintaining it despite the disaffection of taxpayers and the loss of their revenue. The solutions may go further than yet contemplated by Western democracy: the unprecedented political acceptance that government is not able to ensure compliance with its "rule of law."

The obstinate truth is that the growing parallel economy may reflect deeper resentment of taxes that is beyond government influence to discipline unless it withdraws from large stretches of government activity. It may be that the 1997 Government, which shows new readiness to embark on unexpected welfare reform, will find that it will also have to withdraw increasingly from most other services in public utilities and familiar local facilities that no longer satisfy newly affluent families who can find better services in the market.

Whether there is still time, or it is too late because its superfluous functions can be escaped, is considered in Chapter 4. For a Government laudably ready to take advice from scholars researching into the empirical evidence for overdue reforms, employing British economists to emulate Professor Schneider's researches could show whether there is still time.

So far British government has been complacent about the distortions in economic life that will continue if the harmony between government and governed is not soon restored. It will not least entail acceptable relationships between the "official" and the "unofficial" economies. The 2000 figure for the British parallel economy will probably be 10 per cent higher than all other estimates. A total parallel economy approaching 25 per cent of national income is likely unless taxes are reduced much more than now seems probable and regulations are relaxed rather than tightened as implied in the new mercantilist mood in health, safety, rural building, environmental and other precautionary policies.

Non-payers of taxes are increasingly productive citizens. Smugglers, pedlars of drugs, young women from families weakened by the welfare state, and other long-familiar categories, may be increasing. But non-payers of taxes outnumber them as typically self-respecting men and women supplementing taxed earnings by evening, week-end or spare-time services in domestic, secretarial, research work, or sitting with the sick, the old or the young, some paid in cash or by swapping skills and spare time.

An obvious improvement in research on the (illegal) evasion of taxes continues to be neglected. For some years surveys questioned recipients of wages, salaries, fees, fares, tips, and other payments whether or how far they were paid in cash. Understatement of earnings was likely. Surveys that asked payer-employers how much they had *paid* in cash would yield more authentic information (Marjorie Seldon, in Seldon, A. (ed.), *Tax Avoision*).

This approach indicated three improvements on the conventional opinion polls. *First,* it was more reliable since it inquired into the cash paid rather than received. *Second,* it inquired into what the sample had done in the recent past, not into what it might possibly do in the remote future. *Third,* it covered a wider range of work and indicated the range of participants who regard themselves as supplementing family income "in their own time" and would be offended to be categorised as law-breakers.

Such surveys might cause Chancellors of the Exchequer to be less severe in levying taxes. Before long they might find that lower tax-rates yielded higher tax revenue.

Accountants with little training in the elasticities of demand for labour and income may see only the non-observance of government edicts. Economists and political scientists might then theorise on the size of government that maximised the yield of taxes accepted as justified to finance its more modest expenditures. And moralists might analyse the relative responsibility of tax-leviers and tax-rejectors for the strains in government financing and political democracy.

Escape by Barter

The latest form of probably unintentional or unconscious rejection of taxes is the exchange of goods and services, or of goods for services, that arise in the normal course of social relationships between friends, neighbours or members of societies or other associations.

Barter has shown three stages. It was the earliest form of primitive exchange before the use of money. It is a development of informal exchange of services or experience based on custom or tradition among the members of a profession, often medicine, a specialism, possibly engineering, or academic abilities, usually in the social sciences, to share developments in thinking or information from research.

The exchange of services, advice or information is "free" of charge. The intention is mutual aid or stimulus to new thinking. But the unintended effect could be a significant escape of taxes.

The exchange of gestures can easily develop into more systematic organised exchange of goods and/or services that avoid the use of money and are technically barter.

Sooner or later the unintended consequence is a conscious acceptance that both parties are in effect not paying taxes on the monetary value of the income in kind of the goods or services they exchange. The clear result is that the higher taxes are raised the more valuable the informal exchange or formal barter and the stronger the inducement, even if subconscious, to bypass them.

The third development in the unintended non-payment of taxes is the widening use of tokens generally accepted to avoid the inconvenience of arranging exchanges between strangers. People who do not know each other but have goods or services they would willingly exchange can accept tokens. In time the tokens become "money," which is simply a convenient, generally acceptable "means of exchange."

But it is a device which is evidently being found to have wide applications. In the last four or five years it seems to have spread across Britain and attracted the attention of the national newspapers, and most lately broadcasting.

But little is known about how far it has spread. It may well be reaching more parts of the country with new forms of "money." Nor is it clear how it can be stopped if government believes it may one day significantly reduce its tax revenues.

Not least, it is difficult to conclude that even as a natural expression of sentiment between individuals, it should be outlawed by government which upholds the liberty of the subject. For individuals to choose to express gratitude towards one another, even if it impinges on the ability of government to supply so-called "public services," is a seemingly harmless sentiment that government restricts only with risk of disturbing communal harmony. It may set a limit to the amount of individual resources that government can safely claim without forfeiting the public respect on which democratic government ultimately depends.

When at a seminar of economists and political scientists in early 1996 in Yxtaholm, Sweden, the highest-taxed country in Europe, the judgement was ventured that barter could one day become a substantial leakage of government revenue if taxes incited resentment, it was met with incredulity. A highly respected economist from Switzerland indulgently thought it might be an "early shoot" of an economic trend in foreseeable developments in the European Union.

A similar sceptical reaction came from a former British Government Minister at a 1997 conference of liberal economists in Spain. When he emphasised the widely different extents of unemployment between Britain and mainland Europe the "official" figure for Europe of 18 million was described as unrealistic; in view of the double income of the so-called "unemployed"—from unreported employment and national insurance "unemployment" benefit—I suggested that the true total might be no more than 11 million. The exaggeration of unemployment also applies to most of the countries that solemnly submit their official national statistics to the OECD for unchecked republication.

We may never know to what extent the rejection of taxes will evoke a more rapid and extensive resort to barter approaching that of the more common legally-proper tax avoidance leading to illegally-improper tax evasion. If taxes in Britain remain unchanged, or are not appreciably reduced, it must be accepted as a clear possibility that tax rejection will expand to the volume it has reached in the higher-taxed countries of Spain and Italy.

The decisive uncertainty for the future of democracy is its ability—or failure—to rein in over-government to the "optimum" amount that the people are freely willing to pay for in taxes. And here they may prefer not only less to more government; they may also take a chance on too little government that they can expand rather than the too much government they cannot discipline once it takes root.

Escape by Electronic Money

If the relationship of trust between government and people is replaced by growing conflict between over-government and the people's impatient rejection of high taxes, the search for new ways to elude detection by the tax-inspectors and tax collectors may be expected to grow.

Although payments by cash are seen as a way to elude taxpaying, a "cashless society," in which payments are made by electronic "clearing" of debits and credits between banks and other specialists in financial balances, would seem to make rejection of taxes even easier. Such a method of simplifying payments has been discussed by economists in the USA for some 20 years since the Automated Clearing House (ACH) was developed experimentally by the American Federal Reserve as a way to simplify payments.

Its possibilities are still being judged. In late 1996 Alan Greenspan, the Chairman of the American central bank, the Federal Reserve Board, foresaw an increasing rôle for electronic money at a US Treasury conference on the rôle of government in the supply of means of payment. His address on "Electronic Money and Banking" concluded that, although electronic money was likely to play a smaller rôle than that of the private money of currency and cheques, history indicated that government should allow freedom to experiment in the new private currency markets of the twenty-first century.

It is the comparative freedom to experiment in the unknown, even in unknown means of payment for goods and services, that has made the USA the richest country in the world, with far less poverty and inequality than the countries of Europe. Here, except for recent short periods under Erhard in Germany and the then Mrs. Thatcher in Britain, we have retreated to the government-enforced security of "safety first" that makes for indifferent economic performance.

As in other sectors of the economy, industry, trade and welfare, the historic interrelations between government and the market in the inventions of new kinds of money and credit have been misinterpreted. The general inference is that nineteenth-century markets had been inadequate or undesirable and were rightly replaced by government in the twentieth century. This is the precise opposite of the deduction more accurately drawn from the experience of providing private money in America.

The main lesson is that competing private suppliers of private monies had voluntarily evolved rules and procedures that protected the public from the misdeeds of the suppliers of private monies.

The conclusion drawn by Greenspan was that the private market should now not be inhibited by government from refining experiments in providing private monies. The historic truth, difficult for democratic politicians to defend, was that private monies had misled the public far less than US Governments in their debasement of government money by recurring inflations.

The evidence of history until the recent British inflations of the 1960s and 1970s is that the *non sequitur* "market failure, therefore government correction" is still applied to money as to almost every other act of government. Yet "government failure" has invariably been more ineradicable than "market failure."

Greenspan's conclusion in 1997 echoed the rigorous theoretical argument of Hayek in 1976. Ultimately the only certain way to prevent government debasement of its money means of exchange was to "privatise" it. He called it "denationalisation," by which he meant de-monopolisation by transferring it from the sole monopoly control of government to competing supply by banks or other issuers of private monies.

Hayek's "theory" (explanation) of competing monies was impeccable. It supplied the missing link in preventing the supply of money from causing inflation by outrunning the output of goods and services. The sophisticated rules devised by the monetary economists to prevent the over-supply of government money and so inflation relied on the integrity of politicians who had often succumbed to inflation, not least in post-war Britain. After their misdeeds in office they had retired with titles and well-paid consultancies.

But the private suppliers of money proposed by Hayek would suffer financial loss, bankruptcy, public disgrace and worse because their money would lose value if issued beyond the amounts required to lubricate trade and exchange.

Hayek's solution remains the only way to prevent the debasement of government money until, if ever, it is replaced by electronic money.

Scientific advance is now making electronic money more convenient than existing forms of currency in cash or cheque. In the twenty-first century growing disaffection with taxes as payment for unsatisfying government services may lead to further refinements in payment by book entries.

Greenspan foresaw that electronic money would allow payments or banking instructions to be sent increasingly over new networks such as the Internet. It now seems likely that government over-taxing and over-regulation (a major inducement to tax rejection, pp. 119–31) will encourage the invention of new forms of money, electronic and others, beyond cash, cheques, even barter. And law-abiding citizens will use them more as they are refined to serve the four classical functions of money: a medium of exchange generally accepted in payment for goods and services, a unit of account to permit comparison of their value, a store of value that does not deteriorate with time, and a standard of deferred payments.

The essential is that government does not prevent the emergence of new forms of payment. Greenspan argued that private monies should not be prevented from evolving methods of "self-policing" by frequently updated credit ratings and other devices to prevent abuse. The early nineteenth-century experience had shown how markets behave when government rules are not "pervasive" and private suppliers can adapt their trading to changing circumstances.

High-value payments in commerce are likely to be increasingly electronic. But, despite the spreading use of credit cards, everyday consumers still generally pay with paper currency in cash or cheques and are alert to the inflation of rising shop or direct mail prices. It is here that the suppliers of "private" branded monies will come to be seen as more secure than government and its "official" monies.

Government cannot deny its disreputable record of intermittent inflations, even in Britain in our day, and their far-reaching evil consequences. The warning from Greenspan against the financial susceptibility of government is stark:

> I am especially concerned that we do not impede unduly our newest innovation, electronic money, or more generally our increasingly broad electronic payments system.

Escape by the Internet

Intrusive and oppressive government has almost miraculously had to acknowledge a new adversary in the most unexpected technical marvel of the twentieth century.

A recent sample inquiry to the Internet "web" produced around 46,770 "searches" into the "Informal Economy" in countries as varied as Britain and the USA, Mexico and Mozambique. No doubt more would have been found under the range of labels from "black," "shadow," "underground," and many others, though possibly not many so far under "parallel."

Other labels would yield higher numbers. But only a half of word processors are so far connected to the world "Web." The scope for expansion challenges the imagination.

Not least, the latest scientific world marvel of the Internet is advancing at such a speed that it is rash to assess its rate of advance in the twenty-first century. The key will be whether it accelerates faster than the other "escapes" from over-government.

The Internet has been described by Alan Greenspan as "unprecedented in providing versatile, low-cost communication capabilities"—American for simple ways of establishing contact between individuals all over the world. The Internet "web" is the most remarkable technical advance on the two twentieth-century inventions that have revolutionised the means by which strangers communicate—and trade—with each other: the telephone for sound and television for sound and sight. That is the not disinterested view of the most adventurous Internet entrepreneur, Mr. Bill Gates, which seems likely to be as near the truth as that of his competitors. Even if the expansion of Gates's Microsoft product is for a time retarded by opposition to his "monopolistic" tactic of conditional sale with an ancillary component, there can be little doubt that the use of the Internet as a whole will continue to grow probably faster than both the telephone and television.

It will be used in everyday personal life for shopping and entertainment as well as in trading. Every business—industrial, professional, legal, and financial, small and large—could be connected. Young people, even children, are taking to it faster than adults.

By late 1997, one in 10 US adults, 22 million, were using the Web at least once a day; the British equivalent was so far perhaps three million.

The Web will cost time to use to the full, but it will also save time by discovering information almost instantaneously about intending purchases. It will thus raise what Hayek called "the discovery process" of the free market, still often "imperfect," to unimagined heights of "perfection."

No one will have to pay more than the lowest possible price anywhere in the world. For the theme of this Paper no government will be able to charge more in taxes for its services than the market can supply at lower prices around the globe.

That must be a sobering reflection for politicians who still see the national political process as supreme over all other developments. The essential truth they must reluctantly but increasingly accept in the years ahead is that government does not provide the people with a procedure of discovery comparable with the market. Government does not furnish a mechanism by which it can compare or contrast its prices with those of its competitors.

Yet in the early years of the twenty-first century government may be required to acknowledge the truth that its prices are often higher, even where its products are inferior in range of choice, quality, or the failure to refund (tax-)payment if the taxpayer customer is dissatisfied.

That realisation may lead to further public awareness of the inefficiency of government and political acceptance of the sobering truth that government products are worth markedly less than their tax prices.

That may lead to a public demand that government add one final "free" "public" service that will enable the taxpayer to compare government and competing prices. So far the information that central government and its local agencies supply to taxpayers is a mass of macro-economic totals which convey little or nothing of comparative cost and value. Local government taxpayers who are regaled by expensively printed brochures telling of the millions or billions of pounds spent on schools or libraries, refuse collection or fire services, are expected to interpret these impressive strings of noughts as evidence of careful expenditure by wise local Councillors on well-run services. The sobering truth is that they tell local taxpayers nothing of the ("micro-economic") comparative prices and costs of excluded competing private schools or libraries, refuse collection or fire services, which can be lower, especially in Europe or North America. An average-sized county town in the South-East of England proudly tells its taxpayers that it has spent their Council taxes on "vital" or "essential" services (listed in order of amounts):

Housing benefits	£18,214,000
"Other services"	£6,927,000
Planning and economic development	£2,511,000
Recreation and Tourism	£2,344,000
Refuse collection	£1,187,000
Cleansing services (streets and public conveniences)	£1,167,000
Environmental health	£965,000

Local taxpayers would be more enlightened if they could compare the local tax costs/prices of such services with the market costs/prices of competing private services.

The early announcements of the 1997 Government were also mostly "macro-economic" totals. The millions or billions (of pounds) "saved" by the Secretary of State for Health on the "bureaucratic" internal medical markets were transferred to "patient care." The millions or billions "saved" on the Assisted Places Scheme "got rid of" by the new Secretary of State for Education were spent reducing class sizes. Without knowledge of comparative individual costs the claims made for these supposed wiser ways of using taxpayers' money were precarious.

The Internet is more revolutionary than the average citizen knows. Mr. Gates writes his e-mail correspondence on a 20-inch LCD (liquid crystal display) monitor which will be cheap enough in two years to sell to the general public. But in 10 years a 40-inch LCD may be commonplace. Other now unexpected, and perhaps now unimaginable, advances will also then be everyday occurrences. And scientific advance will have removed the Web to safety from the police control or restrictive regulation of political government.

So much for the view of a producer. A graphic but authoritative account of the spreading Internet by a discriminating consumer is no less mind-stretching. The distinguished American journalist, Andrew Sullivan, has eulogised his "wonderful web life." The Internet has become not only "an economic or scientific event [but] a genuine cultural shift" by reaching "a critical mass of users . . . accessible to all."

That stage has been reached in competitive America. It seems slower to reach corporatist Europe. The resistance to technological innovation is natural for established industrial, managerial and employee interests in Europe that may be disturbed by them. Yet economic advance is brought to life by the open market and can no longer be suppressed by government.

The advantages of the Internet for humanity are disturbing to the conservative mind, which invariably ignores the benefits that would be lost—to the poorest as well as the richest. Mr. Sullivan dramatises them as a user newly awakening to its potential. The most popular Internet service, America Online, is used by more young and middle-aged people (aged 17 to 49) than listeners or viewers of network news programmes.

It has created "a new era." He, and many like him, communicates more by e-mail than by telephone. He "e-talks" to his family, doctor, editors and stockbroker. . . . The world's [news-]papers are "delivered to my screen, free. I chat with strangers. . . . Who [he may offend his British opposite numbers] needs pubs?" For £60 his computer camera and video software enable him to talk live with anyone with the same technology anywhere in the world.

"Once you've bought the equipment, usage is free. I haven't bought a book in a bookshop for a year. Every possible title arrives at my door within two days. . . . I sent my mother flowers with a click [on his personal computer]. . . . I buy airline tickets, socks, no longer write cheques, pay bills, taxes. . . . I can buy stocks for £6." Who, the British investor may ask, needs a stockbroker for £100?

The wider economic and political benefits foreseen by this graphic observer are even more dramatic, if perhaps more arguable:

> The full consequences . . . [include] the immense boom in the American economy. . . . When information is as accessible as this . . . the world shucks off an ancient barrier to communication . . . growth booms, prices fall. . . . It's capitalism by keyboard.

"Capitalism by keyboard" is a dramatic slogan that the defenders of Western capitalism, long cowed into silence by the century since Marx and Engels, could now use in harmony with Yeltsin.

Many observers may remain sceptical of such awe-inspiring technology. It savours of the "irresponsible" activity outside the ordered political arrangements with foreseeable consequences created by the rule of law of the political state. But it may prove to be the most liberating technology invented in the twentieth century with unforeseeable expansion in the twenty-first. Its anarchic structure, says Sullivan, "is the most striking testimony to America's capacity to generate new commerce and culture from the chaos of freedom."

"The chaos of freedom" comprises the institutions that permit the politically unrestricted entry of new buyers and sellers to meet and enrich each other in free markets.

This vision illuminates the economic conditions that permit the emergence of unpredictable change, advance and progress. It is the debilitating failing of the non-economist who does not understand that all progressive human life emerges from unavoidable uncertainty. It is the crippling effort of government to introduce "order" that excludes avenues of discovery, advance, progress, with rising living standards for all, from the poor to the rich.

Mr. Sullivan's "*chaos of freedom*," rarely understood by the critics of the market, dramatises the system of free exchange between individuals that explains the innate power of free markets to produce progress. And it explains the unavoidable fate of "ordered" society produced by the over-government of socialism and social democracy to degenerate into loss of freedom and lagging living standards.

"Chaos" theory is a development in economic thinking that is revolutionising the natural sciences. It explains how the apparently unforeseeable fluctuations in human reactions, which seem irregular, reveal broadly regular predictable trends. The human reactions emerge by a process of learning from the experience of uncertainty. Human beings who know their immediate circumstances more than outsiders learn to adapt themselves to the uncertainties of life better than political authority can enforce by regulations. It is simplistic to suppose that uncertainty can be foreseen and controlled "in the public interest" by centralised, short-termist, biased political judgement.

In America the Internet, says Mr. Sullivan, has opened up a new frontier "of complete democracy and limitless anonymity" in which the individual is not subject to crippling law framed by irresponsible, uninformed "democratic" politicians. He is now empowered to "reinvent himself not merely twice in a lifetime but [on the Internet] *twice in an hour*" (my italics). People can "renew" themselves as often as they can "change their [Internet] screen name."

Government will crib, cabin and confine the human spirit no longer. In the Internet

> there is no government; and, as yet, no taxes. As Britain fast becomes the second country to join this Hayekian [*sic*] paradise, Britons may soon discover they are getting more than a convenient way to check on their stocks. They could—virtually—enter the [same] state of anonymous nirvana.

It is to be expected that national governments, perhaps in league with other governments, will attempt international regulations to maintain knowledge and influence, controls and restrictions on these developments. The more likely trend is that science and the human spirit will remain two or three decisive steps ahead of the slower-moving machinery of international politics.

Escape to the World

In the history of mankind the world has providentially offered escapes from poverty and oppression. In our times the New World of North America remained "New" to the peoples of "Old" Europe whom it welcomed or accepted in their desperate search for relief from the poverty of Tsarist Russia or the savagery of National Socialist Germany.

These escapes required the risks and fatigues of moving families of young and old from "Old Europe" to unknown lands and homes in "New Europe." The New World of science that empowers individuals to escape from ignorance and poverty faster than ever in human history now offers the people of Europe easier escape. They require no physical movement or cultural risks experienced by their forebears.

Within Europe the free trade of the new Union offers escape from national governments that would limit freedoms of trade. The outlawing of hand-guns in Britain has been diminished by the ability of the citizen to escape by joining gun clubs in nearby France without moving home. More such escapes will limit the power of national governments to destroy the freedom of their citizens.

There is now increasing escape from British government services of all kinds, not least medical care, insurance of all kinds, even education and housing.

The latest domestic, home-bound "New World" that science has opened out in the last two decades could raise world-wide living standards even faster. It has vastly accelerated the rate at which the simpler telephone and radio of the early and mid-twentieth century began to link Old Europe with New Europe without moving hearth and home.

The recently formed Union of Old Europe has virtually freed the citizens of the nation states of Europe from the danger of internal friction from political nationalism and economic protectionism that disfigured Europe after the First World War. The danger remains of protectionism against the outside world. Better than the European Union would be a North Atlantic Union of Old and New Europe in which all the nation states in both Continents renounced trade barriers between themselves.

If a North Atlantic Union is not formed the political powers of the nation states of Europe will be escaped by the resort to trading by electronic money, barter or the multiplying new devices that ease the rejection of oppressive national laws and invasive taxes.

CHAPTER 4

From Political Democracy to Individual Liberty

Democracy at Bay

The cordial relationships between democratic government and the people as voters, customers and taxpayers have deteriorated.

The power of the people in democracy has grown in their three roles as citizens.

- As voters they are the ultimate rulers who no longer have to accept representatives who fail to interpret their interests.
- As consumers they can increasingly reject government that produces services they no longer want.
- And as taxpayers they can increasingly escape paying for services they reject.

Democracy as it was developing with individual, family and spontaneous group initiatives has been misled by political democracy into over-expanding the small sector of necessarily collective association. The people can now increasingly escape from them, but government cannot withdraw them because of the obstruction of its beneficiaries.

The political process of democracy has impaired the power of the people to learn from experience in protecting themselves from both irregular, unquantifiable uncertainty and recurring insurable risk. This is the historic failure of democracy: it has prevented or discouraged the people from learning from the discovery process of the market. It has confused the few services that for a time may have required to be collectivised in the state with the many which could better have been personalised through the market.

Democratic over-government is now belatedly rediscovering the mechanisms of personalised insurance that the people were discovering and developing but the state irresponsibly discouraged and almost suppressed until growing incomes, technology and tax rejection compelled it lately to confess failure and abjectly appeal to the people to resume the self-propelled private insurance proliferating in the market.

The New Mercantilism

Democracy is searching for new solutions to avoid over-government. The latest is a variant of the medieval mercantilism in Europe from the early sixteenth to the end of the eighteenth century.

The medieval notion of the supposed advantages of exporting more than importing in order to produce inflows of gold money developed political coalitions in later (sixteenth- through seventeenth-century) Parliaments that are echoed in the present-day advantages, claimed by politicians and academics, for linking state and economic life in a "third way."

Government that paternalistically regulated the detail of industry seemed to work more or less harmoniously with the early merchant venturers. The "system," analysed by the Swedish economist Eli Heckscher in his masterly 1931 study, *Mercantilism,* was soon abandoned when, as with all national "planning," it became too centralised and rigid to suit the rapid pace of the Industrial Revolution in the new vigorous markets of the late eighteenth century.

The classical economists especially revealed mercantilism as inadequate to facilitate faster economic advance. Adam Smith's *The Wealth of Nations* in 1776 was essentially a powerful intellectual and philosophic broadside against mercantilism. And it eventually gave way to the inadequate and short-lived yet powerful 40 years of freer trading in the mid-nineteenth century.

Recent developments have seen a new liaison between historically hostile state government and private industry. The great debate of our times has been on the relationship between government and market, between political power and economic law, the power of government resting on law and the power of the people to better their condition in competitive markets.

The 1997 Government echoes the mercantilist anxiety to advise, admonish or regulate the details of industry for "the public good." Four conflicts of interest emerge.

First, government power over the conduct of industry can restrain the instinct of entrepreneurial minds to react promptly to market opportunities at home and overseas. The political mind cannot absorb the flexible reactions suited to the economic potential of the future. The predictable regularity in the "chaos" of free scientific invention can be discovered only by the market.

Second, imposed conditions of employment in hours or rates of pay in industry, or other politically convenient acts of mercantilism, conflict with the interest of the owning shareholders who provide the savings for capital investment. Small shareholders, now often from working-class backgrounds, will look to the expertise of the institutional investors to protect them from political promises that cannot be honoured.

Third, government that increasingly hopes for private monies to rescue its failing projects, not least state education, must expect to pay exceptional yields for the exceptional risks of enterprises run by "public officials" with no experience of the skills acquired in competitive markets.

And, *fourth,* the false trail of vaguely defined external "stakeholders" conflicts with the interest of the owners—from wealthy shareholders to small investors in unit trusts, life assurance or lately ordinary shares in "mutual" organisations—who risk the loss of their savings.

All these interests are reconciled in the market, which outlasts its politicised alternatives because no one can easily escape the services of the state but all can stay with or exit from the market at will. As a political coalition the market is inherently unstable. If it were kept together by the coercive power of the state it would intensify the instinct of all parties—investors, shareholders, managers, workers, consumers—to escape from its regulations and taxes.

All "stakeholders" would see themselves as rivals for the goodwill of the state. Such a contest for political favouritism was feasible in the slow-moving mercantilist times. They would soon succumb to the age of ambitious scientific, industrial or financial innovators.

Too Late to Withdraw

The central question is whether democracy has indulged political importunity too long to be able to resist the barnacles and other obstacles to its withdrawal from over-government.

Winston Churchill retorted to the post-war mood of "freeing the colonies": "I am not here to preside over the dissolution of the British Empire."

Government will now find not only that it must relax its economic empire. It must, more humbly, accept that it has lost the power to maintain it. The escapable power of political government meets the irresistible economic force of the market.

The remaining decision is to arrange its retreat with dignity before the escapes multiply to deprive it of the authority to influence the rate of its withdrawal.

The power remaining to government turns on the ability of politicians to recognise their weakening influence. Before long there will be increasing public understanding that the expansion in the state over the decades was unnecessary. The possibility must remain that the ability of government to command the economy can be by-passed not only by crudely breaking its laws and refusing its taxes, which recent evidence indicates may grow. The more constructive reaction would be to open markets everywhere: that is the only way to produce, much faster than political machinery, the new goods and services expected by the increasing numbers of rising incomes.

Government production may have coped with annual prewar rises in real income in some years of 1.5 per cent, doubling every 40 years, or the post-war 2.5 per cent, doubling in 25 years. It will be no match for future annual 4.5 per cent rises doubling every 15 years.

The people have rarely been able to determine what government "should" do by awarding or withholding their votes. They can now more fundamentally decide what government can do by supplying or denying taxes and taking spending decisions outside its powers.

The Solution

Democracy has finally confessed it has lost the power—and moral authority—to finance (pay for) its inferior, dispensable, low-quality, outdated services. Its politicised "public" goods, its politicised public "utilities," its politicised "social" services, its politicised local authority services: all have to be subjected to the test of the market if they are to continue.

Government validated by the test of the market in the twenty-first century would satisfy the seventeenth-century Thomas Hobbes who left the long-taught warning that the excesses of the over-zealous sovereign were likely to be less malign than the mayhem of society without government. The twentieth century knew the excesses of over-zealous government in the brutal dictatorships as well as in the benign welfare states.

Economists have long sought to discover the forces that determine the size of government. Several have left legacies of the solution that seemed important in their times.

The German Adolf Wagner in the late nineteenth century saw government as intent to increase its weight as national resources expanded. The British Professor Alan Peacock and his collaborator, the late Jack Wiseman, in 1961 traced over several decades the increases in government authority during wars but the reluctance to withdraw when peace could dispense with its increased powers. The American William Baumol in 1967 saw government as intent upon enlarging its proportion of the national product in order to maintain its "public services" because its productivity tended to fall behind that of the private sector. And the American Professor Gordon Tullock in 1967 emphasised the growing power of pressure groups—"rent-seekers"—to extract increased expenditure from democratic government.

These, and some other, theories explained some or much of the growth of government in the periods when they were evolved. The emphasis here is on the recent increases in the influences—including rent-seeking—making for over-government and the even more recent increases, or hitherto under-emphasised expansion, in the "escapes" from over-government.

It is their recent confrontation—between escapable power and irresistible force—that has brought the new inability of government to maintain its supremacy over the market and provoked the dilemma of democracy.

The warnings of philosophers have not always been wise. Thomas Hobbes's warning was inadequate. His *Leviathan* declared that without sovereign authority there could be no state. Twenty-first-century democracy will have to rule with modest authority that reflects the general will. Without such reticence no legal authority will ensure popular observance. To echo Benedict de Spinoza: the sovereign has moral authority to exercise legal power so respectful of its subjects that they regard rebellion as worse than obedience.

PUBLIC CHOICE IN BRITAIN

CHAPTER 1

Public Choice or Political Sovereignty?

The Insights of Public Choice

Public choice has developed many insights into the economic motives of politicians and the economic consequences of their political powers—by laws, rules and regulations, taxes and charges—to direct or influence individual lives.

Professor Tullock explains that "people are people," subject to the same motivations in (so-called) "public" life as in their private lives. This economic view of human motivation contrasts with the flawed view of political science which presents human beings as behaving very differently. They are then seen by many political scientists and sociologists as acting selflessly in "public" life and selfishly in private ("commercial") life.

The analysis of "public" choice has revealed that this distinction is a fallacy that has led to far-reaching error in the study and conduct of "public life" in government. Even more, it has revealed the damaging effects on human liberties of the *over*-government generated by the system of "democracy" in which the people have allowed themselves to be ruled by the representatives they elect hopefully to safeguard their interests.

Economists' deepening examination of "public choice" in collective decision-making by government has revealed fundamental contrasts with decision-making by people in buying and selling as individuals, families, voluntary/spontaneous groups, firms or other units, in the day-to-day exchanges of markets.

The difference between the two systems of decision-making is fundamental and far-reaching. People exercise their decision-making in the political process as voters, in the market process as consumers. Public choice is

As explained in the Introduction to this volume (p. xiv), "Public Choice in Britain" was written as Part III of a book, Part I of which was written by Gordon Tullock and Part II by Gordon Brady. There are references in the text to these other two Parts.

the relatively new study of the second-hand collective preferences or opinions of the people as voters in the political process in contrast to their first-hand individual preferences and choices as consumers in market exchange.

The questions that the political process does not answer are: How far should voter preferences outweigh consumer preferences, and in which goods and services? The economic process of exchange solves the question of how far consumer preferences shall prevail.

Collective and Individual Decision-Making

By the end of the three Parts of this Readings it will become apparent to newcomers to the subject that the distinction between collective and individual decision-making is the often ignored key to the very different consequences for living standards, personal liberties in all aspects of life, and the prospects of amity in national and international relations.

It will also have emerged in all three Parts that the term "public choice" is a misleading name for a system of economics and politics in which the choices of the real public are not generally satisfied by the political "public" institution of collective decision-making. The ultimate truth is that the politicised "public" institutions are not primarily concerned with the choices of the real public as individuals or families.

The essential reason is that collective decisions are made by representatives of the public, not by the public themselves. The indirect results that emerge in the politically-decided production of goods and services are usually very different from those that would be chosen directly by the public itself.

The working of "public choice" in principle is presented by Professor Tullock in Part I and illustrated in Parts II and III from its working in real life in Anglo-American countries. Dr. Brady illustrates public choice in Part II from government policy on the conduct and rules governing industry in the United States. Part III examines the working of public choice mainly in British "social welfare" and allied services. The analysis helps to explain why collective choice displaced individual choice for over a century in much of industry in the USA and in most of "welfare" in the UK. It thus also shows why, in both countries but especially in the UK where collective choice has advanced further than in the USA, government has finally outlasted its utility in much or most of both industry and welfare, and why it will be increasingly replaced in the twenty-first century in both countries as incomes rise and technological advance supplies services more suited to individual preferences.

The British welfare services discussed are mainly education, medical care, housing for people with low incomes, insurance against interruptions of earnings in sickness, unemployment and retirement, and protection against everyday risks.

Government and Public Goods

The increasing displacement of collective by individual decision has changed the focus of interest in democracy and revealed the continuing *over*-government it has generated. So far, from the end of the eighteenth to virtually the early twenty-first century, the political debate between leading economists has centred essentially on the necessary or desirable functions of government. These were generally thought to be the "public goods" that it was supposed only government could supply. The focus has now to change from the necessary or desirable functions of government to the *incapacity* of government to limit itself to the necessary or desirable public goods. The central debate in politics and economics is moving from what government "should" do to what it *can* do when people find better services outside the state. And the long-apparent necessity to move large tracts of earnings from individuals to government by taxation or other means is being increasingly questioned.

The fundamental distinction is now increasingly between which services government *should* provide, which has been the long-lived concern of political science, and those it *can* provide when there is rapid advance in economic life and government functions can be replaced by superior services in markets. What government can do is increasingly decided by changes in the two fundamental components of economic life—supply and demand—which the political process often ignores at severe cost to the people. What government should do—how large or small it should be—was long debated by the opposing schools of economic thought which argued that it should do as little as necessary or as much as possible.

The English economist J. M. Keynes clarified an essential difference in the thinking on the functions of government—that it should do only what the people could not do at all, not what it could do better than the people.

The caution was timely when he wrote in 1932 (in *The End of Laissez Faire*[1]) but it has been largely ignored in the last 60 years by politicians in their anxiety to achieve or maintain power. What government began to do in social welfare and elsewhere in the last decades of the nineteenth century it was rarely ready to abandon even when, in the twentieth century, individuals showed they could do both more for themselves and better than could be provided by government.

The New Distinction — What Government Will Be Able to Do

The new distinction in the functions of government in the twenty-first century—what it will be able to do—is even more fundamental because it weakens or removes from government the power to continue with many services it has long thought to be its essential functions. So far government has persisted in supplying—and extending—supposedly essential services begun in the nineteenth and twentieth centuries. They were standardised for all, or increasingly most, of the people and ranged from the mediocre in quality to the blatant denial of personal choice. For the mass of the people with lower incomes there seemed no alternative. Increasingly since the 1950s, even as incomes rose and technological invention accelerated, standardised state services were continued when more people could obtain services that better suited individual and family preferences.

The standardised state services became increasingly inadequate. Yet until recently there seemed to be no escape for the millions of people with the lowest incomes. In the new century the increasing power to buy better than the state can supply, and the general dissatisfaction with the standardised state, will accelerate.

Reluctance to Pay for State Services

Moreover, there has been increased parallel reluctance to pay for state services indirectly by taxes or directly by charges. In Britain the illusion that

1. J. M. Keynes, "The End of Laissez Faire," in D. Moggridge (ed.), *Keynes: Collected Writings,* vol. IX, Macmillan, 1972, 272–94, was heralded by the politically minded as a far-seeing tract for the future. Since the 1939–45 World War it has been increasingly rendered out of date by technological invention that has raised incomes and enabled people as consumers to replace government as producers. The much-neglected evidence has been analysed in Arthur Seldon, *The Dilemma of Democracy: The Political Economics of Over-Government,* Hobart Paper No. 136, London: Institute of Economic Affairs, 1998 (reprinted in this volume).

the state has the infinite resources and the supposed moral duty to supply "public services" whatever their quality, their denial of individual liberty, and their costs, long fostered by politicians and sociologists, has paralysed public discussion and scholarly thought. In recent years other methods of payment for services exchanged privately between individuals and groups have, moreover, appeared on a growing scale in the form of barter and in the replacement of office or factory by home working (a twentieth-century advanced form of the "domestic system" of the eighteenth century) based on the new range of computers, word processors and the latest telecommunication devices. This shift in the work-place is accompanied on much larger scales by electronic money and Internet transactions between strangers in unknown countries and continents.

The distinction between tax avoidance and evasion in the methods of paying for government goods or services, whether sanctioned or disallowed by the law, became blurred. Increasingly, in the last 15 years, the state has begun to lose the power to raise the funds required for its stubbornly continued personal welfare services, especially education, medical care and housing, all of which have failed to keep pace with the rising quality and standards of food, clothing, domestic comforts and personal amenities bought increasingly in open markets by people with lower but rising incomes.

The latest phase in the retreat of government is for state schools to ask parents for voluntary donations or gifts of equipment. The state hospitals have long looked to patients' families and friends to provide secondary "non-medical" comforts and facilities. Government housing is increasingly outdated by new homes that the state cannot match. And government in Britain can no longer assemble the funds required to fulfil its undertaking to supply acceptable income in the predictable or unpredictable vicissitudes of life—sickness, unemployment and ageing.

The Failure of State Welfare Services

The general trend is that democratic government in Britain is failing to maintain the range and flexibility of its welfare services in comparison—and therefore competition—with supplies available in the newest shops and stores in town and country. The increasingly everyday evidence of outdated government supplies and services, and therefore in the very rôle of government, raises the crucial issue for the politics of democracy: When will representative government have to accept that it is not competent to cope with the opportunities and expectations of the future?

Insofar as there are industrial, political and cultural similarities between the United Kingdom and the United States the observations on each country in Parts II and III apply to the other. And, insofar as such differences persist, the vital task of the real "public's choice" is to ensure that government reflects private preferences. The people of Britain have yet to emulate the power of Americans to create the political mechanisms that reflect their individual preferences. On both the supply and demand sides of economic life the American economy is far advanced over the British. Personal incomes in the USA are about 2.25 times those of the UK, and the economy is much more competitive and productive because producers in all states know they can specialise within the federal market of 275 million consumers rather than the UK market of 59 million. The political power of federal and state governments in the USA to deny private preferences did not advance as far as that of the increasingly socialising policies of the British central governments of all parties—Conservative, Liberal and Labour—over the last century. And the much larger markets of American industry over the 50 states have enabled Americans to escape from over-government into private exchange more readily than in Britain.

Voting Systems and Voters' Preferences

The fundamental elements of public choice analysed in Part I—the fraudulent voting system that frustrates rather than faithfully reflecting voter preferences, the pursuit of rent seeking, the rewards of logrolling, the self-interested bureaucracy, the chronically excessive taxation, and the failure to confine legislation to its irreducible "federal" economic limits—will be seen at work in the large parts of the British economy in which government persistently provides services which are clearly personal and family, though misleadingly described as "public" or "social."

These characteristic features of representative democracy have had fundamental but often undesirable effects on the British welfare services. The precarious voting systems of "democracy" revealed by Professor Tullock, and demonstrated in Part II and below, do not, or cannot, faithfully reflect the preferences of voters. A passing temper of impatience among voters with a government, as in Britain with both political parties in 1979 and 1997, can produce a large change to its opposite rival for many years, much longer than the days or weeks required to change between shops. Undeclared logrolling between representatives in the British Parliament who know little of one another's special interests, which they may even think harmful, enables them to serve their personal political interests at the expense of unsuspecting voters. Rent seeking by British voters organised predominantly as producers—in recent years typically miners, teachers, railway workers, state health or local government employees mobilised in national trade unions—has extracted undeserved privileges at the long-term expense of unorganised consumers. The ignored irony in this producer pressure on government is that the victims are often themselves as consumers.

The Power of the Bureaucracy

Not least, strategically placed bureaucrats, better-informed than their political masters, advise the adoption of policies that fundamentally serve their bureaucratic interests or reinforce their prospects by organising voting pressure. In view of the large numbers of government staffs—from administrative and electronic through medical and pedagogic to clerical and manual organised in professional associations and trade unions—the question raised by Professor Tullock, whether "public officials" should sacrifice the right to vote as an improper influence on their employment interests, will before long have to be faced in Britain.

Populist causes—disguised as the sanctity of "public services"—are used by government to justify taxes otherwise rejected or resented by taxpayers. Government has been inflated beyond its optimum limits. It should be decentralised and confined to its irreducible boundaries.

CHAPTER 2

Government Intentions and Consequences

The Economics of Politics

"Public choice" is the academic name for the analysis of the powers and decisions of government made for the supposed good of the people. A better description is "the economics of politics," for three reasons. The *first* and most obvious is that analysed by Professor Tullock in his Chapter 1: with rare historical exceptions, political power does not transform people into selfless saints or all-wise seers. The *second* is the less obvious reason, still generally overlooked or denied by political scientists and sociologists, that elected government (or any other collection of individuals) cannot judge the individual preferences of the people it is designed to represent. And the *third* is the historic evidence that, even where the collectives begin by putting the people first, they end in putting the people second and themselves first by continuing their activities long after economic change has made them undesirable, superfluous and resented.

A crucial purpose of public choice economics is to analyse the motives of individuals in government—as politicians, their advisers, "public servants," senior bureaucrats and their aides. It identifies their objects and functions as men and women in "public" life and reveals whether, if at all and how, they differ in contrast with the objects of individuals in "private" life.

Public and Private Purposes

Professor Tullock concludes from his analysis of public choice that human motives are fundamentally the same in public as in private lives. The supposed contrast between public and private purposes is largely fictional. People in private activities, who work in competitive markets, have to do real public good because if they fail they can be more easily and sooner deserted by escape to competing suppliers. There is no such ready escape from political government. People in public life claim to act selflessly in the interests of "the people"; but in practice they put their personal interests first.

The word "public" is among the most abused terms in the English language, certainly in politics. The study of public choice reveals its misuse. The London School of Economics economist, Frederick Hayek, who built the powerful 1930s fusion of classical English/Scottish and Austrian liberal thinking, wrote in his last book, *The Fatal Conceit,*[1] of the confusion produced by the frequently-used but question-begging term "social." It was often carelessly employed to imply selfless activity for the benevolent "general good" in contrast with the private individual activity that is supposedly designed for selfish personal, "commercial," advantage.

In Britain, much the same distinction has been conveyed by social scientists in their simplistic contrasts of "public" with "private." The insinuation is that "public" means selfless or benevolent whereas "private" means selfish or greedy. Hence the emphasis on the benevolent and desirable "public interest," "public service," "public expenditure," "public investment," "public enterprise," and a range of services from "public transport" to "public libraries." It is the most misleading word in the vocabulary of politics, where it is even more question-begging than "fair," "reasonable," "appropriate" or "just." The politician who wants to sell a doubtful policy he cannot explain or justify calls it "in the public interest"—or by the nebulous "fair."

Moreover, "public" blessings are contrasted with the opposite self-interested and therefore undesirable "private interest," "private service," "private expenditure," "private investment," "private enterprise," "private transport," "private libraries," and many more.

The implication is that objectionable "private" activities are in principle—when chosen, produced, and distributed by supposedly disinterested representatives of the people in legislative assemblies—superior to the goods or services chosen and preferred by the people themselves and obtained by voluntary private exchange and trade.

The distinction is patently false. Yet its falsehood has been suppressed by the persistent teaching since the eighteenth century of the precarious proposition that representative political assemblies know more about the condition of the people who elect them—their wants, "needs," preferences—than the people know themselves.

1. F. A. Hayek, *The Fatal Conceit: The Errors of Socialism,* London: Routledge, 1988, and Chicago: University of Chicago Press, 1989.

A Fictional Distinction

The verdict of history in Britain—in the final consequences of the welfare state and its "social" welfare—does not support the fictional distinction between "public" and "private." It may be convenient to allow representatives in Parliament to organise some services for a time—perhaps years, some as long as decades—until individuals can supply them better for themselves and one another. In Britain there were some such necessary or desirable "public goods"—from defence to "public health" precautions of the growing industrial towns—even in the period of *laissez-faire* free trade in the mid-nineteenth century. But the historical evidence shows that once the representatives exercise government control of "public" services they do not vary them with the ability and desire of the people before long to supply them for themselves. "Public goods" tend to become permanent even when people can arrange them better privately.

In Britain what should have been a few years of political control were stretched into centuries. There is no formal British parallel for the American "sunset" industries or public services that are ended when they become superfluous. In Britain, it seems, once a "public" service always a "public" service. At the turn of the nineteenth to the twentieth century no less than half of them could in time have been transferred to free exchange between individuals and firms—the remaining so-called "basic industries" like fuel and transport, certainly most of education and medical care, all "Council" (local government) housing, most pension saving, insurance against interruption of earnings by industrial adaptation to changing technology, and most of local government services. Many are still kept as "public services" by the political influence of the rent-seeking trade unions and professional organisations.

Politicians and the "Public Interest"

The claim of British politicians to serve the public interest is, with few exceptions, baseless. The theory of the superiority of public over private services is both a myth and an internal contradiction. It is a myth because in the real world it is not safe to allow political representatives to exercise outdated powers to provide "public" services. British history reveals that in the long run the people would have been better advised to discover new private ways to produce and distribute goods and services that are used jointly than to run the risks of almost permanent, inefficient, wasteful control by political representatives. If they are better produced jointly, people long ago would have found new ways to produce them jointly in voluntary, flexible organisations without the use of political representatives.

The Myth of Collective Superiority

There is a conceivable condition in which individuals cannot or will not move to produce a service unless all agree and all pay. The obvious case is defence against external danger. But that is hardly likely in personal services such as education, medical care, homes or insuring against interruptions in income like unemployment. These "welfare" services satisfy intensely personal requirements that vary widely with individual circumstances or preferences. And all can be bought from suppliers who provide services to suit individual requirements. Moreover, as incomes rise, and state services such as education and medical care in Britain today deteriorate, more families will pay for them by school fees and health insurance. The myth of collective superiority is being gradually destroyed by changing supply and demand in open markets. The claim that welfare is a "public good" is being abandoned.

The notion that political representatives can serve the people better when people become more capable of dispensing with them as their incomes rise is even more implausible. In the course of economic development, such as that since the late eighteenth century, incomes of all the people—from the richest to the poorest—have risen unexpectedly fast. The rise was not uniform down the years or similar in all income groups, but the general movement has made the children of one generation much wealthier than their parents and especially their grandparents. As life-expectancy has grown with improving health by the conquest of disease, especially in recent decades, the 25-year generations have grown to 30 years. The children have become twice to three times as rich as their parents. Few "working-class" British people would now choose to live in a government-built Council house. They would much prefer a refund of taxes or a housing voucher with which to choose a home, a health voucher with which to avoid long queues for doctors, medicines and hospitals, an education voucher to escape from the worst state schools, as they now use luncheon or travel vouchers from their employers to choose meals or means of transport.

Returning "Welfare" to the Private Sector

The obvious conclusion is that, as national income rises, the state can return its few unavoidable "social" welfare activities to private welfare suppliers. That could have been the history of British life since the last war. Political power has fanned the naïve notion that, as national income rises, the state should demand more of it to spend on public services. It seems to have escaped social historians that national income has increased because personal earnings have been raised, mostly by individual effort and enterprises, making much state activity superfluous. The state could be reducing the taxes it raises for outdated activities, leaving the citizen with the added advantages of widening choices in satisfying personal requirements.

CHAPTER 3

Over-Dependence on the Welfare State

It is a severe reflection on university teaching of the social sciences in Britain that the lesson for policy-makers and their servants was lost in the political theology of the welfare state. That rising family incomes could reduce the writ of the state, and with it the power of politicians and their servants over private family life, has rarely been discussed, or even contemplated, by enthusiasts for the welfare state.

In spite of the broad historic progression in incomes and living conditions the opposite notion, common among well-meaning supporters of the early social services, was that they should be extended on the apparently obvious ground that, as incomes rose, the tax revenue of government would also rise. This apparently generous impulse has been revealed as a simplistic *non sequitur.*

The LSE and Enlargement of the Welfare State

At the leading centre of British university scholarship in the social sciences in the inter-war years, the London School of Economics (LSE), the thinking of the Founders (Beatrice and Sidney Webb) and their ardent Fabian followers encouraged the view that higher private and therefore national incomes should enlarge the functions of the state. The *non sequitur* escaped the Fabians and their successors. This simplistic teaching was rejected by the liberal school of economists at the LSE nurtured by Edwin Cannan and later led by Austrian-born Friedrich Hayek and the British Lionel Robbins, with their gifted younger teaching colleagues, not least J. R. Hicks and R. H. Coase, both, with Hayek, eventually Nobel Laureates. Yet the *non sequitur* has lingered in the teaching of social sciences in British universities generally where it has spread from the LSE.

The truth is precisely the opposite. For several post-war decades after 1946 the welfare *non sequitur* persisted at the London School of Economics with re-emphasis under the sociologist Richard Titmuss. More recently it has been revived under another sociologist, the new London School of Economics Director from Cambridge, Anthony Giddens, who claims to have discovered a nebulous "third way" between political and private choice, the state and the market, which the economist scholars who built the 1930s LSE would have scorned as losing both—the fading advantages of the state and the growing advantages of individual choice.

Rejecting the Fabian Fiction

By chance a foremost independent thinker of the Webbian-Fabian tradition declared its tragic errors in early 1999. A Church of England journal published his historic rejection of the Fabian fiction as Part III of this *Primer* was being completed.[1] He has now emerged as the rare social scientist, with personal experience of developing a benevolent lobby for children, elected to the status of a government Minister in 1998, which he abandoned when he found his revisionist thinking did not suit the philosophy or short-term intentions of the 1997 government. He described his challenging magisterial theme on the welfare state as "What, Then, Was Unthinkable?" His testament, a reasoned rebuke to his political friends, vividly illustrates the working of public choice in practice.

In Part I, Chapter 3, on "Logrolling," Professor Tullock recounts his surprise on discovering on a visit to England in the 1970s that British parliamentarians, including a former Cabinet Minister, were apparently not aware of logrolling in day-to-day Parliamentary practice. He learned from a Member of Parliament that members of the House of Commons generally and habitually exchanged voting support for one another's attempts to introduce legislation in which they were personally not involved nor even personally interested. This was logrolling in the Mother of Parliaments.

If, presumably, no money changed hands, British logrolling was the exchange of services by barter, which elsewhere facilitates the escape from taxes. But its importance was more general and questionable.

The lack of knowledge—or state of ignorance—by British voters of logrolling between Members of Parliament remains to this day. The exchange of voting might support or oppose Parliamentary permission to build roads

1. Frank Field, MP, in "What, Then, Was Unthinkable?" *Crucible,* published by the Board for Social Responsibility, Church House, Westminster, London SW1P 3NZ, 1998. All the quotations in the discussion that follows are cited from the above source.

or other large-scale structures that could be worth millions of pounds to pressure groups and their lobbies. They may be seen as innocent or possibly harmful, even, in the technical sense analysed by Professor Tullock, "immoral." They may be as innocent or as immoral as evidently practised on a large scale in the USA Congress 100-member upper house Senate and the 435-member lower House of Representatives.

The "thinking-the-unthinkable" declaration is that of Frank Field, for several months Minister of Welfare Reform during 1998 in the 1997 New Labour Government. His long experience as a pioneer in formulating social policy for children in low-income families has led him, after his recent painfully short term of office and resignation, to formulate new thinking on the fundamentals of welfare policy. The central theme is how the welfare state will have to be changed fundamentally to reflect the latest developments in rising incomes, family life and attitudes to paying taxes.

Mr. Field's clearly presented text reveals the historic change in his approach to the political practice of public choice—the collective supply of welfare by government—analysed in this Primer. His latest thinking elaborates the new policies—a combination of private and state arrangements for supplying income in unemployment, sickness and other conditions—that must now replace the mistaken Fabian-Titmuss philosophy of "higher incomes therefore more social welfare." And it raises the most fundamental dilemma in human existence, examined by economists analysing the future but not always by other social scientists overwhelmed by the past, that the prevailing universal scarcity of resources, finally recognised after decades of self-delusion, requires government to confess that more given to some people means less available for others.

"Titmuss believed," says Mr. Field, "that we were on the threshold of abundance," the unknown condition in which there is plenty for all, so that more for some does not reduce what is available to others.

> "In an age of abundance," Titmuss argued, "the production of consumption goods will become a subsidiary question for the West. . . . Welfare could be delivered by government to all citizens free of conditions and obligations. . . . universal welfare services could help establish a basic equality between individuals."

This was the fatal Fabian fallacy in thinking on the welfare state. In setting this goal, said Field, Titmuss "followed the political tradition of R. H. Tawney [the highly-respected Fabian socialist scholar] whose ideas about equality sprang from his view that . . . men and women were created equal." But, continued Field, "the age of abundance was still far off. *Welfare was still a scarce good.*" (My italics.) Given human nature, individuals were likely to respond more carefully if the benefits they were drawing had been earned and were not presented as a free good. The truth at last. Hallelujah!

"Altruism," Field warned, "might be expressed within small groups such as families or very close friendships. But it was not a motive on which the institutions of wider society could be safely governed." Frank Field has bravely declared the emptiness of a century of Fabian fable.

These "institutions of wider society" are the collective services and institutions supplied "free"—the state schools, universities, hospitals, homes and much else—built by government elected by representative democracy. They are the benevolent institutions long advocated as universally the task of government. But in the real world, as analysed by public choice, human nature is not more benevolent and may be less benevolent in public choice than in private lives. Electing men and women as representatives in government, or appointing men and women as "public" officials, does not transform them into saints or seers. The thinking of representatives and officials, said Field:

> was that universal provision was possible only through a state-run scheme. [But] only by *separating* the need for universal provision from a state monopoly [will] it be possible to extend the universal ideal.

Separating Universal Provision from State Monopoly

This is the separation that British politicians in all parties are now in the twenty-first century having to re-examine and confess in abject humility. But most still cannot wholly accept the abandonment of the welfare state because it implies confession of a century and more of political irresponsibility and intellectual error. The longer it is prolonged the more severe the error since 1946–48 when the welfare state was last expanded by the post-war governments.

"The reality running through much of this revisionism," continued Field relentlessly, in the modern dilemma of over-government "under-funded" by a reluctant tax-paying people, "was an attempt to come to terms with the public's attitude to the payment of taxes and the receipt of services."

"There was," he added with the candour still unfamiliar among his former political colleagues, "and there is a resistance to the payment of taxes, yet there continues to be a demand for high quality public services." A most fundamental change had taken place in the electorate's views.

Why? "A number of factors were at work. . . . Rising living standards have increased the resistance to the tax-take on incomes."

And here emerged the truth long concealed by the Fabian teaching at the London School of Economics: "As real incomes have risen, so too have the choices open to individuals on how that income might be spent. And these are the choices that *individuals themselves increasingly want to make.*" (My italics.)

"Instead of merely railing against this change, thinking the unthinkable was about accepting it as the framework within which the development of welfare should take place." Field added, to his old friends: "The challenge . . . was how to make the promise of universal service compatible with this new set of voter preferences."

But, as the analysis of public choice indicates, the next step would be politically delicate because it would reveal the unwelcome truth—the underlying philosophic and political reluctance of recent British governments to lose their power to run the state.

"The aim," said Field, "was to show how it was possible, with the restraint taxpayers now imposed on policy-makers, to achieve an adequate universal provision of pensions." His solution was "to form a partnership with the private and mutual ['not-for-profit' in the American term] sectors."

This is the new blasphemy in British politics that the 1997 government, reluctantly and cautiously, is having to approach and embrace. But even more fundamental reform will have to be contemplated. The emerging task was "how best to police welfare expenditure," that is, to ensure that the newly recognised scarce resources were spent with due regard for the economic theory of marginal returns to displaced alternatives: that to maximise the use of tax revenue the marginal utility (usefulness) in alternatives used would have to be equalised so that £100 million spent on "free" schools would do at least as much good as £100 million withheld from "free" medical care.

Tawney, Titmuss and Unlimited Resources

The fundamental Tawney-Titmuss fiction of unlimited resources has been, and still is, influential. The 1940–45 war-time all-party government led by Winston Churchill accepted the 1942 Report on Social Services prepared by Sir William Beveridge, the former Director of the London School of Economics, in the 1930s. He had also been in 1911 adviser to the then-Liberal Ministers, Lloyd George and Winston Churchill, on the first national insurance scheme, financed through the state by "social insurance contributions" and taxes. Here, Field rightly says,

> what was surprising was that Beveridge [in 1942] seemed willing to ignore so many of the lessons he had learned over the previous 40 years . . . like the Webbs and most of the reformers he was intrigued by the startling social advance by so many of the skilled working class during the late Victorian and Edwardian era

from the 1880s to 1910.

The vital truths staunchly faced by Frank Field, more than by any politicians or academics in the new 1997 government, recognised the improving conditions in working-class life as the source of the errors made by those who urged the expansion of the welfare state. Their guilty failure was to overlook the massive progress in working-class living standards and the associated mechanisms for voluntary working-class insurance that were produced, not by the politicians in the political process using the force of law but by private individuals in the market helping the people to help themselves.

The Failure of Social Historians . . .

It was the failure of the social historians to recognise the origins and extent of voluntary insurance that falsely validated the unnecessary—and flawed—state insurance system. It has finally damaged democracy, and is now intensifying the dilemma which arises because it has expanded too far and cannot withdraw for fear of losing its political supporters. But it is being increasingly escaped by the same people as consumers and taxpayers. "The engine of such social advance," records Field, "was located . . . in the friendly society movement." These were the voluntary "mutuals." It was here in the early twentieth century that the newly-formed Labour Party made the first of its many mistakes in defence of its then members in the working-classes.

Field withdrew in 1998 from the government formed by his political party because, as an independent-minded thinker, he put what he saw as the real world of human beings in families before the requirements of government anxious to maintain public popularity by avoiding disliked reforms.

It may now be clear why "public choice" has been redefined in this section of the *Primer* as "the economics of politics." The new Secretary of State for

Social Security, Mr. Alastair Darling, saw public choice as "the politics of economics." Professor Tullock's outline of the principles of public choice in Part I suggests that government Ministers may justifiably see their task as, above all, to maintain their government and political party in office even if they put last the policies that would best serve the long-term interests of the people.

But the new Labour rebel against the Fabian fallacy now puts the long-term interests first. He speaks of "downsizing the state." This is the fundamental classical liberal view that as incomes rise the state can do less. It would have been political blasphemy in the previous Labour government when in power in 1974–79. Remarkably and courageously he now urges his political friends to accept that "the only sure foundation for welfare [is] to build on . . . the natural impulse in most of us to look after ourselves and those we most love"—by which he means essentially the family.

The historic testament by Field enforces reflection on the economics of government—of frustrated "public choice" in its literal sense—that permitted the wide contrast between the changing personal and family circumstances of the people and the forms of government they had allowed to develop and tolerate over the past 150 years.

. . . and the Failings of Democracy

Field's final thought—that people must be allowed to put first those nearest to them—reveals the failure of democracy. The question remains what the new policies are to be. The new circumstances of the twenty-first century make them very different from those of the late nineteenth century. The working people of those years from the 1880s may have done their best with voluntary societies. Their increasingly middle-class children and grandchildren will now want to use all possible mechanisms for insurance against loss of income and will want the most efficient, whether private or state, "for-profit" or "not-for-profit." That means they will want to use the techniques that make for fastest progress—the competitive market and its full range of the latest advances in communications and in methods of payment, not least those that minimise tax imposts.

That is the structure of representative government produced by political power that will resist change and has finally provoked the "*Dilemma of Democracy*."[2] Democracy has now grown too far beyond the acceptable

2. A. Seldon, *The Dilemma of Democracy, op. cit.*

functions and services of the state that the people once accepted because they could not provide better themselves by market production and exchange. But economic and technical advance create new "escapes" from outdated government by tax rejections, informal domestic and business exchange/trading and other devices that are difficult for government to trace in the growing parallel economy, ignored by most social scientists.

Beveridge's Error

Beveridge's error was, surprisingly for a Liberal Member of Parliament, that he under-estimated the extent of the expansion in what Samuel Smiles would have called "self-help." The extent of pre-First World War voluntary working-class social insurance was much larger than Beveridge had revealed in his 1942 Report. In the 1972 IEA historical study, *The Long Debate on Poverty,* on the misleading writings of Charles Dickens and other "state of England" novelists who distorted fact to write fiction, Dr. Charles Hanson, the economic historian at Newcastle University, revealed the error was still being made in 1947.[3] I had gone to consult Beveridge, as a fellow-member of the Liberal Party, on technical details of state pensions. I found him writing *Voluntary Action,* his apologia or lament for the demotion of the voluntary societies from insurers to administrative agents of the 1949 state insurance. But he was still under-estimating their coverage. Dr. Hanson found that, by omitting the unregistered friendly and other voluntary societies in 1947, Beveridge had failed to discover that only a small minority of working men had not yet insured against sickness and old age by 1909.

By the first year of the twenty-first century the error on voluntary insurance is now the opposite. To strengthen his case for extension of "social" (state) insurance Beveridge, in 1942, says Mr. Field rightly, had "exaggerated . . . the inadequacy of voluntary insurance." In the new century the new aspirations of the higher-income working people will urge them to seek out the most efficient and fastest mechanisms, whether "public" or private. They will supplement the best of the "not-for-profit" organisations by the newest with shareholders who will insist on the most efficient directors and mechanisms. The obstacle will remain that the economics of politics in democratic government, the process of "public choice," will induce democracy to

3. C. G. Hanson, "Welfare Before the Welfare State," in A. Seldon (ed.), *The Long Debate on Poverty,* IEA Readings No. 9, London: Institute of Economic Affairs, 1972, pp. 111–39.

over-emphasise the risks of human life in the twenty-first century, as it had done in the twentieth.

The evidence of British history is still foreign to the social historians and the sociologists. It is that the main services of what became "the welfare state" suffered from three crucial defects in disregarding the changing conditions of the people:

- They were introduced *too soon* by false argument and before the private mechanisms could show their superiority.
- They were maintained *too large* in forms that did not respond to or reflect individual private wishes.
- And they were continued *far too long* when they had become superfluous because the people could provide them privately with better regard for individual preferences.

Experience demonstrates clearly that the "public choice" delivered by government contrasts, sometimes moderately, often sharply, with the private choices of the people. Knowledge is discovered continuously down the centuries, sometimes slowly, often quickly. Knowledge has developed in free societies by teaching personal skills that encourage individuals to benefit and enrich each other, or often one another, by exchanging knowledge of skills and eventually goods and services. In time they learn to concentrate (specialise) on the skills they acquire most easily. They move on to pure barter without money, then learn to use portable or durable objects in common use as money. They eventually end by separate stages of buying and selling in places, at times and in markets that suit them best.

Transferring Social and Welfare Services to the Public Sector

Most of the goods and services now described in Britain as "social" or "welfare" began to be bought and sold by exchanges in markets from the early 1800s. In the past 200 years continuing advance in technology and sciences would have refined the scientific and exchange mechanisms. By now, and advancing rapidly in the 2000s, the British would have developed specialisation and private exchange between individuals, families, and small groups of the goods and services now falsely called "social" or "welfare."

Unfortunately, excuses for transferring them from private people to "public servants" were found. The private services—especially education, medical care and pensions—were condemned by social historians as growing too slowly: they were rejected as providing for only small numbers of people. Only government, they said, could accelerate their growth to cover most or all of the people.

From around the 1870s the political process of electing representatives in government to supply "public choice" was developed by both the Conservative and Liberal parties. And once the goods and services were transferred from "private" to "public" they were expanded and made comprehensive and eventually became established and unquestioned parts of national life.

It is historic fiction to argue that these services could not be expanded to satisfy more of the people but had to be supplied—or supplied better—by the political process and elected government. The tragedy for private personal lives is that, once captured by the "representative" collective organisations, with their falsifying voting, rent seeking, logrolling, and the rest of the paraphernalia of "public choice," ordinary people were denied the methods of production and distribution, and buying and selling developed by private barter and exchange down the centuries.

For 130 years since about 1870—since the Gladstone-Forster Education Act of that year—people have been seduced into accepting the fiction that if left to their lowly life-styles, low incomes, and passive acceptance of authority they would neglect their families and themselves. They would not pay school fees or insure for medical care; they would live in mean housing; they would risk poverty in old age.

So the 1870 Education Act introduced "free" government schooling even though three in four working-class children had attended private fee-paid schools (paid by parents assisted by the church and charities) since 1860 and earlier. In 1911 the Social Insurance Act coerced into state insurance 12 million working-class male employees when nine million were covered by Friendly Society and other private insurers. In 1921 local authorities began building the council housing that deteriorated into the slums and later high-rise tower-blocks in which their tenants' children will not wish to live. And in 1949 the post-war state pensions were enlarged but in 1998 were found inadequate for an increasingly affluent populace.

The Harm Done by the Welfare State

The final irony is that the welfare state—ostensibly created to better the people in most need—has done most harm. The welfare policy that was being outdated by irrepressible long-term economic advance has been prolonged by short-term political patching-up of services that have been found wanting and are being rejected by the people as inadequate and outdated. In Britain recent governments have been spending large sums of taxpayers' money to patch the buildings—and retain the staffs—of schools, hospitals and institutions that are becoming outdated. And in the most recent government only one Minister, Mr. Field, a close student of British society who became a politician, has spoken the inconvenient truths—and lasted only a few months in office. "Public choice" in the political process has never represented the real choices of the real public.

CHAPTER 4

The Weakening of the Family

A consequence that clearly follows from the tenacity of the welfare state is the weakening of the British family by the continuing displacement of parents by political agents.

Historians give it scant attention in their accounts of social policies. Sociologists have only lately confessed government errors in policy affecting the family—faulty money grants, mismanaged local authority homes for the neglected aged, the lonely single mothers, the abused children removed from families into "public" institutions in which they were supposed to be safe, and mismanaged local authority homes for neglected grandparents.

Separating Children from Parents

Yet few, if any, historians or sociologists trace the effects of the over-long century of state welfare services that separated the natural links of dependence and affection between parents and children. Through peace and war, boom and slump, summer and winter, decade after decade, the mass of British children has been accustomed to accept that their parents have little competence and virtually no influence on their schooling, their medical care by doctors and nurses, even for perhaps 10 million children on their homes. To ensure money to feed them through sickness and unemployment, they would in vain look for comfort from their working-class parents. Ninety-five children in every 100 were confined to state schools, often the nearest one round the corner. Many or most might be attended by local doctors employed by the state that replaced the Friendly Societies or other working-class insurance organisations. Perhaps a quarter of families lived in Council houses built by local governments which their parents could not improve.

Children saw these elements in private family lives as supplied by strangers over whose activities their parents had little or no influence. Even worse: the poorer their parents, the weaker their cultural influence in pleading for better attention to the vulnerability of children with exceptional difficulties. And, worse than all the disabilities, the poorer children in the better state schools were displaced by children brought into the area by new higher-income residents who had moved to acquire the residential qualification required to use the local "free" state schools and avoid paying fees for private schools. The parents, such as Mr. and Mrs. Blair, were doing their best for their children but at the expense of poorer children.

The strangers who replaced parents were often the members of the rent-seeking trade unions of teachers and professional associations of officials whose main purpose was to extract higher pay and better conditions from their local government employers rather than to satisfy parents that their children were educated to their satisfaction.

The usurpation of the authority of parents by "public servants" weakened their family authority in other aspects of private and family lives. Not least was the observance of rules of personal conduct. The unwritten laws of the "respectable working-classes" that I saw around me in the pre-war East End of London were being increasingly broken, often scorned, when post-war sociologists replaced parents as the teachers of civilised behaviour. The broken homes and personal unhappiness that followed the disparagement of marriage ignored the increasing evidence that children were happiest in households with two parents.

The dangers seem to have been seen by the new 1997 British Government: hence the emphasis of its March 1999 budget on easing the taxation of the conventional two-parent family. But there is a long way to go before the coherence of the family is restored by a revolutionary restoration of children's confidence in the capacity of their parents to ensure their well-being in the fundamentals of private lives.

Displacing "Public" Officials

The ultimate solution is nothing less than the displacement of "public" officials, "public servants" and "public" employees by the revival of the authority of parents to reject inadequate schools, crowded medical centres, and captive housing, and by empowering them to pay fees, medical insurance and rents or other costs. This is what parents will show they prefer as their incomes rise. Since many own homes with rising values that could produce neglected funds, they need no longer leave their children in the "free" but no longer acceptable state schools or allow their lower-income parents to wait months or more for "free" hip replacement or cataract surgery. The advancing "working classes" may find new ways to pool their resources to strengthen family lives in defiance of the state that weakened them over the decades.

Public choice analysis reveals that the real public has little real choice precisely in the most personal services created by its representatives in government. The acceptance by politicians that they cannot satisfy the diversified requirements of the people—above all in education, medical care and their own homes—is the indispensable condition for the rejuvenation of British family life.

CHAPTER 5

Voters Versus Consumers

The analysis of public choice reveals, much more than conventional political theory, that collective choice-making in government has made the fundamental error of putting the vaguely identified interests of the people as voters before their clearly perceived interests as consumers. This historic error results in providing them with standardised services, supposedly to suit hundreds or thousands, or hundreds of thousands, or millions, rather than individuals or families in different circumstances with diverse preferences.

One-Size-Fits-All Services

The difference is between a tailor who supplies "off the peg" one size, or six or 20 sizes, for thousands or millions of people instead of "bespoke" sizes for each individual or family. Even where individual differences are deeply personal, the political process herds people into a few large pens in which they are treated as more or less equal or identical.

The suppression by government of individual judgement of the risks in everyday living is perhaps the most insensitive invasion of deeply individual liberty, where politically standardised treatment can do most harm.

Exploiting the Fear of Risks

Governments in Britain (and other democracies in Europe and North America) have exploited the human fear of risks in many regular or occasional decisions and purchases in everyday life. So it has offered "help" in many forms, from advice to prohibition, in anxieties about loss of income in sickness, unemployment, old age and others. The new British Government is now going further, in paternalist or medieval-mercantilist manner, by arranging standards of quality or precautions against uncertainty in a lengthening list of goods and services—food, clothing, motor-cars, homes and many others.

Its effects have varied from helpful to harmful. But its purpose has varied from winning popularity at elections to raising revenue in taxes to pay for services in which there is no public choice, and in principle no rejection.

Its most recent purpose—to raise taxes—reveals its fundamental internal tensions. Lately in Britain, perhaps because the 1997 government has exhibited increasing anxiety to protect consumers from imperfect or dangerous goods and services, the populace seems to be losing its faith in official advice. There is a new conflict between official advice from "public" authorities and "public" confidence in services chosen—or rejected—by individuals. A reason may be the accusations of critics that the goods and services at risk are those produced less by public-spirited "public servants" than by "profit-seeking" commercial companies. This distinction is difficult to maintain since the bulk of public complaint is directed to state-produced goods and services—poor schooling, inadequate medical care, poor housing. At the time of writing the most urgent public anxieties are directed at suspected unsafe foods. Here the evidence of national sample polling, imperfect though it often is in discovering "public" opinion, reveals unprecedented loss of confidence in political judgement.

The findings may reflect the experience of disease evidently transferred from animals to humans in the early 1990s, but lately of special interest since the relevant poll was commissioned by the new government-created Better Regulation Task Force, in the praiseworthy task of assisting Ministers in "managing risk."

The object—to judge where to allow individual choice of risk and where to empower government to ban risks for all—seems laudable. The findings, which may be premature, seem to be that the politicians were not trusted by the public in judging where individuals could be left to judge risks themselves. They revealed a wide gap between the risks in foods publicised—or exaggerated—by politicians and as judged by scientists and other "specialists." The percentages of members of the public who reported anxiety conflict widely with the evidence of the scientists (see table opposite).

Clearly, public choice analysis indicates that politicians will not act strictly on scientists' findings. They will play safe and avoid the risk of blame for public anxiety at all costs. They will exaggerate the risks and hope to maximise the political goodwill. This is cheap political prudence since they can conceal the costs (taxes) of widespread precautions in masking the risks

Risk	Public Anxiety	Scientific Evidence
1. Pesticides	69% (women)	No hard evidence
2. Genetically treated foods	57%	GM foods probably safer than many conventional foods
3. BSE in beef	54%	Beef probably safe — no effects for years or decades
4. E. Coli	94% aware of risk 25% sense risk	Affects one in 46,000 in England
5. Salmonella	99% know the risk 51% sense the risk	Infection uncommon, rarely life-threatening
6. Camplyobacter	13% know the risk	Illness rarely fatal

Source: *Daily Telegraph,* 8 February 1999.

by complete prohibition of production or sale of the suspected substances. Suppressing the costs of insuring against the risks by well-publicised outright prohibitions is clearly preferred by the politicians. They stand to gain public goodwill at little or no cost to themselves in running government.

Yet it may be that people will, in the end, win the test of influence with the politicians. Government values people as voters more than as consumers. And the polls indicate increasing sophistication by the people as consumers (and producers) above their former selves as voters (and taxpayers).

The essence of the finding is not that government servants could not judge the chemical or other suspect content of risks in food. More fundamentally, the political objection is that politicians were not elected to judge risks collectively for the people as a whole, rather than allowing individual people and families to judge risks for themselves.

Restraining Political Paternalism

Slowly, very slowly, the public is summoning its courage to tell politicians to restrain their self-interested paternalism—and in these days of increasing numbers of women in politics and especially the 1997 Parliament, maternalism. For to politicise the precautions against possible risks in food, and much else, is to pay scant respect to the common sense of the public and its better ability to judge whether the risks apply to those who take care in their choice of suppliers.

The government supervision of quality—in almost medieval-mercantilist detail—is an unseen cost of public choice that inflates the powers of "representative" democracy which does not represent the better individual judgements of the people.

CHAPTER 6

The Political Fate of Economic Federalism

Decentralising Government: The Case in Principle

The purpose of federalism, outlined by Professor Tullock in Part I (and in his book, *The New Federalist*[1]), is to decentralise government and its political power as far as feasible to the smallest possible political authority which would be best acquainted with local circumstances and requirements. The economic result would be to leave the maximum possible amount of local economic activity to agreement among local individual residents or groups, and the minimum possible to control by the politicians.

The ideal outcome would be that economic functions—the public goods proper that could not be supplied by agreement between private individuals or groups—were performed by the most appropriate size of political governments. The supreme public good of prevention of friction or war between countries would be delegated to a small joint federal office, leaving most other functions to constituent countries and their local authorities.

Centralisation in Practice

The reality has been very different—in some countries almost the opposite. In the USA, and to a lesser extent in the other federal unions, Canada, Germany, Australia, political power has become more centralised because political decisions have been yielded to the federal government.

Public choice analysis, the economics of politics, reveals the main reasons for this disappointing outcome. In the light of this experience there is understandable anxiety in Britain about future developments in relationships with the countries of mainland Europe. For the British people this would be an unprecedented reform with undemonstrable advantages and unassessable risks. The analysis of public choice suggests probable developments in political structures and economic results that affect opposing arguments.

1. G. Tullock, *The New Federalist,* Vancouver, BC: The Fraser Institute, 1994.

For the student of the economics of public choice the essential interest lies in the extent to which government creates the optimum size of political authority—centralised or decentralised—for the optimum economic functions. Professor Tullock has illustrated the optimum centralisation and decentralisation in the government provision of public services. Federal government is best confined to the few functions—the "public goods"—most efficiently supplied from the federal centre for the "federal" country as a whole. The more varied functions are best supplied by local agencies of government at the periphery which can take into account divergences in economic conditions and human preferences.

The Real World of Federalism

This is the ideal world in which political institutions are more, or, ideally, precisely suited to the varying geographical extent and similarity of economic functions. Here as elsewhere the ideal world and the real world differ widely. The real political world of federal systems has produced functions more centralised and more extensive than they need be and than the peoples would prefer and could create in free markets.

For the USA Professor Tullock has illustrated the many services that are better because they are more localised than in Britain. At the other extreme the US Federal Government has, over the decades, taken into its centralised control services that were once better controlled by the individual States.

The dangers of over-centralisation were seen in the creation of the Interstate Commerce Commission with the function (among others) of outlawing barriers, requested by importuning rent seekers, and created by State governments to exclude "imports" from other States. This aspect of internal trade in the USA—its tendency to impose protection from other "countries"—is analysed in principle by Dr. Brady in his discussion of "protection."

The Protection of Industry

The protection of industries was a growing feature of trade between the nationals of Europe until the First World War. One of the few arguable but plausible excuses exploited by Hitler in the Second World War was his complaint that the 1932 Ottawa Agreement excluded Germany from markets in Africa. It was one of the glories of the liberal school of scholars at the London School of Economics in the 1930s, led by Robbins and Beveridge and including names that should be remembered by the British people—F. C. Benham, A. L. Bowley, T. E. Gregory, J. R. Hicks, W. T. Layton, Arnold Plant, G. L. Schwartz—that in their 1931 testament, *Tariffs: The Case Examined,*[2] they openly deplored the abandonment of free trade and the adoption of protection. They signed their manifesto of faith in free trade by a declaration that echoes the nuances of the English language:

> we should all think it a disaster, if the policy of Free Trade which has served Britain so well materially, as through her it has served as an inspiration to all who in any land have worked for good understanding among nations, were today to be sacrificed to ignorance or panic or jealousy or specious calculation of a moment's gain.

One more reason for the growth of barriers to trade between individuals, families, firms or other private buyers and sellers emerged after 1931. The introduction of protection taught rent seekers in Britain and elsewhere that they could generate wealth for themselves more easily by importuning government to impose protection—by tariffs, quotas, and other devices—than by producing goods and services wanted in open competition by the general population of consumers. Thus came about the modern growth of the rent seekers, whose origins, effects and damage to living standards are analysed in Part I by Professor Tullock.

Why Centralisation?

The important question is why the units—states and others—comprising countries called federal unions have allowed political power to become more centralised in the federal government rather than remaining decentralised in the separate units. Professor Tullock has indicated the economic advantages of decentralisation. The task for the economist is to explain why the economic advantages of decentralisation have been sacrificed in politically-inspired federal centralisation.

Here the economics of public choice offers explanations far superior to the unconvincing reasoning of outdated political science. Public choice is in essence based on the science of economics in everyday life transactions between real individuals or groups of people. Political science is largely limited

2. *Tariffs: The Case Examined;* the authors were chaired by Sir William Beveridge, then Director of the London School of Economics, Longman Green & Co., Second and Popular Editions, 1932.

to the study of the artefact machinery created by their supposed representatives in government. Economics dissects the advantages to individuals and groups in co-operating by purchase and sale of each other's goods and services—or lately on a small (but increasing) scale by barter.[3] Political science is largely limited to the study of the machinery of political government control over what would otherwise be private lives.

The tendency to centralisation of political influence in the North American Federal authority in Washington is of interest to the peoples of Europe. In Britain the focus of concern is how far economic integration in Europe will be exploited by the familiar fatal propensity of politicians to inflate their powers by centralising economic functions in larger units of political government approaching federalism.

Differences Between the USA and Europe

A comparison and contrast between the economic tendencies in the USA and Europe indicates similarities and differences that may explain, though not necessarily justify, the differences in economic development and structure.

The "new Europe" in the USA was created largely by Europeans from "old Europe," but their economic and political developments have differed widely. Average income in the USA is 2.25 times that in Europe largely because of the size and the variety of the area in which there is internal freedom to trade, and therefore much wider scope for the specialisation ("division of labour") that, Adam Smith taught in 1776, is the secret of the production of wealth. The instinctive sense of Americans in all States, from the architects of the Union in the 1780s to the present day, was that the freedom to trade with the peoples of all other states in the union was the secret of creating a federal power that could prevent the parochial-minded state politicians from impoverishing the States by preventing inter-State commerce.

The acceptance of the USA Federal Union was also easy for the immigrants from Europe who since the early seventeenth century came from different countries—Holland, England, Scotland, France, Germany, Italy, Russia, Poland—yet who could accept one another as culturally comparable minorities. They soon learned that the wisest course was to exploit the differences between their skills and exchange their resulting products.

Great Britain was also the product of different, although only four,

3. A. Seldon, *The Dilemma of Democracy, op. cit.*

peoples: originally the English (formerly mainly Saxons and Danes) and the Welsh, in 1707 the Scots, and in 1922 the Northern Irish. They are now, at the meeting of the twentieth and twenty-first centuries, decentralising some economic powers, mainly to the Scottish and the Welsh, but remaining a British, economically "federal," union for joint services: defence, law and order and, so far, the social services of the welfare state. The intention was that joint functions would remain in the "federal" (not so described) government in London. But many determined Scots want more power, exceeding the limited power to tax they now have, to act as an independent state in Europe.

The uncertainties, and anxieties for many British citizens, are how far economic union in Europe to ensure its original purpose—free trade to raise living standards—will evolve into a politically Federal union in which economic power to create, control or regulate working lives in Britain and the other countries in mainland Europe will be exercised by a "Federal" government in Belgium or Luxembourg, with main institutions such as banking in France or Germany. Public choice, the essentially economic analysis of politics, is therefore a better guide than political science in assessing the probabilities.

The prospect for higher living standards in Europe with free trade has for some time been creating and multiplying producer interests that will organise as rent seekers to lobby the Federal authorities in mainland Europe even more than they have the national governments of their separate countries, and perhaps even more persistently than their long-experienced opposite numbers in Washington.

The further unknown is how far the combined countries of Europe may be tempted to act as a larger economic entity in its "protective" relationship with the politically separate countries in other continents. A discouraging precedent is the recent abandonment by the once protectionist USA of its newer free trade mission in the World Trade Organisation.

European Producers and Rent Seeking

In Europe organised producers—in both employers' associations and employees' trade unions—have been learning the arts of rent seeking. The European Members of Parliament will be learning the arts of logrolling. The Ministers in the proposed European Union have been weighing the advantages of acting as national patriots against those of "inter-national" European statesmen. The Common Agricultural Policy (CAP) will have taught the lessons of rent-seeking tactics and strategy. And the ruling Commissioners of the newly United Europe have lately been accused of the personal abuses of power familiar in other federal unions.

All these short-run calculations will be at the long-term expense of the interests of all the people—often ironically the same people—as individual and family consumers. Europe may emerge on a larger scale with the over-government that treats people cynically more as voters to enlarge the powers of the political masters than as the loyal servants of sovereign consumers.

These powerful (because immediate) short-term political impulses will contend with underlying long-term economic liberalism. The peoples of America retain fading European cultural loyalties of one or two centuries. The still nationally separate peoples of Europe continue with the cultural differences between North and South, East and West, of a thousand years. The uncertainty is whether the culturally-conscious people of Europe will accept as much Federal authority from Brussels or other capitals of the European Union as did their families who emigrated to America and are now proud of their second, third or fourth generations ruled from Washington.

Attitudes to Paying Taxes

Acceptance or rejection of government is fundamentally seen in the attitudes to paying taxes as they exceed acceptable limits and invade personal ability to raise living standards by mutually beneficial trade. There is a wide and decisive difference between accepting taxes with resignation and rejecting them with defiance. Professor Tullock has adopted a new term, "tax avoision," for the mixture of legal avoidance and illegal evasion that tends to merge in law or is difficult to distinguish in moral content because government may be more immoral than the people if it imposes taxes that do not reflect their willingness to pay.

The official statistics of the national governments in Europe cannot be accepted as accurate measures of public approval. The experience of most individual countries reveals that the official figures of incomes, saving, employment or unemployment are vulnerable as measures of public approval. The official OECD figure of 18 million unemployed is a caricature of the real number of Europeans who may be officially "unemployed" but are busy earning sizeable sums in all kinds of "unofficial" work to keep their families in acceptable comfort.

And the more Europe is "federalised" the less loyalty can be expected in the payment of European taxes or observance of European laws, rules or regulations. If the Italians, the Swedes or the Scottish resist taxes imposed in Rome, Stockholm or Edinburgh, they are hardly likely to be more scrupulous in paying taxes imposed in Brussels or Luxembourg.

Supplementary budgets, from annual to quarterly, to raise the missing revenue will multiply. Declarations of national revenue and expenditure at meetings of the G7 and other assemblies will become even more fictional.

The Rejection of Democratic Government

Democratic government is being rejected by more conventional methods of exchanging goods and services: from minor local forms of barter to larger-scale exchange of surplus stocks between sizeable companies. Electronic money in international exchange is also easing informal deals between strangers never likely to meet. These and other new means of exchanging valuable information or advice—commercial, legal, political, technical, medical and more—enable more people to bypass the over-arching intrusions of growing federal government. The assumption that governments supply services that are necessarily desirable is being questioned the more extensively they invade personal and family lives and the further they are from day-to-day activities—from local, through regional, to country-wide and federal origins.

Two conclusions follow, both from public choice analysis. The better prospects for the people, in their fundamental capacity as controllers of the use to which their resources are put, lies in the combination of economic system and political structure that places their economic authority as consumers in open markets before that as producers in the political arena. That authority will require a constitution that empowers them as taxpayers to discipline politicians by denying their taxes more than as voters who can less effectively deny their votes.

Escaping to Open Markets

The decisive conclusion is that the power of politicians to frustrate the people is not measured by the weight of legislation but more by the ability of people to escape from it in open markets. And the escapes are more numerous in federal systems misused to impose centralisation than in decentralised country, regional, and local government. Escapes are more numerous still in open market daily exchange between individuals who know one another's wants better than do "public" servants.

CHAPTER 7

The Escapes from Over-Government

Political Power Yields to Economic Law

Before Buchanan and Tullock, the pioneer economists who initiated the invasion of politics by economic principles and revealed its pretence of devising the most democratic (because most representative) form of government, there were students of politics who sensed its limitations and dangers. But they fell short of analysing its structural imperfection and excesses.

Some Forerunners of Public Choice

Pierre-Joseph Proudhon, the mid-nineteenth-century French philosopher, but a weak economist, went too far. "To be governed," he warned in 1857, "means that at every transaction one is registered, taxed, priced, licensed, authorised, reformed, exploited, monopolised, robbed: all in the name of public utility and the general good."

"Public" utility is the misleading description used by the political process to disguise the economic source of its superfluous services. Proudhon failed to distinguish between the unavoidable and the unnecessarily collectivised "public goods" analysed by Adam Smith. Proudhon revealed his weak economics by listing pricing as an excess of government. It is largely the failure of government to price its growing services other than public goods that has produced over-government.

John Stuart Mill, the mid-nineteenth-century economist, anticipated the claim that government would or could breed necessarily selfless benevolent politicians. Four years after Proudhon, when the two political parties, later labelled Conservative and Liberal, were contemplating a widening franchise from which they would extract increasing political support, Mill sobered expectations. Although he sat in the House of Commons as a Liberal for a few years he counselled:

> the very principle of constitutional government requires it to be assumed that political power will be abused to promote the particular purpose of

> the holder . . . because such is the natural tendency . . . to guard against which is the special use of free institutions.

But such "guarding" has not proved adequate in the century and a half since Mill. Constitutional (that is, representative) government has not protected the people against over-government. The old fallacy that only government can provide "public services" has unnecessarily prevailed for a century or more. It lingers ironically in the British Liberal Party which was supposed to have disciplined over-government in its heyday of power in the late nineteenth century. After the March 1999 budget its financial spokesman, sadly a Scot who has probably not heard of Adam Smith, lamented the failure of the government and the Conservative Opposition to raise taxes in order to expand "essential public services."

It was left to the early-twentieth-century Austrian economist (and Finance Minister), Eugen von Böhm-Bawerk, to foresee, in his long 1913 essay, "Macht oder Ökonomisches Gesetz" [Political Power or Economic Law][1], that government could and would over-reach itself by supplying services—not least education and medicine—that the citizens with rising incomes in the late twentieth century could and ultimately did reject and escape in growing numbers. That is now the new trend in the function and content of representative government.

The Problem of Over-Government

It is nearing 40 years since the joint Buchanan-Tullock economic analysis of public choice revealed the unavoidable flaws in the belief that government should supply services that the citizen could buy in the market. The implication of the economic analysis of government is vital for the future of democracy and the rule of law. By its congenital failure to avoid over-government, and by inflating its powers and laws beyond the irreducible and therefore acceptable powers of government, democracy has endangered the rule of acceptable law.

The analysis of public choice can best be seen as the conflict within human beings in their functions as voters and consumers. Individual men and women do not consume simply what other men and women have produced. They produce what other men and women want as consumers. The study of public choice has revealed the fatal flaw that the political process has tended

1. Eugen von Böhm-Bawerk, "Macht oder Ökonomisches Gesetz," first published in *Zeitschrift für Volkswirtschaft, Sozial Politik und Verwaltung*, Vienna, 1914.

to pursue its own interests in siding with the people as producers rather than consumers.

Yet, as incomes rise, the primary power of the people lies increasingly in their economic ability as consumers to subordinate themselves as producers. The sad evidence of history is that the over-government produced by representative democracy has for a century and a half in Britain subjected the primary economic interest of individual men and women as consumers to their secondary economic interest as producers.

The Weakening Grip of Government

This power of government, especially since the end of the 1939–45 World War, is being radically weakened and undermined by changes in both arms of economic life—supply and demand. All human life is subsumed under one or the other. Demand is being gradually but massively transformed by rising incomes, changing methods of trading and exchange from selling and buying to barter, and the increasing use of electronic money. Supply is being dramatically transformed by technological advance, the move from office or factory to home, and the world-wide web. Trade between buyers and sellers has long been conducted between strangers linked indirectly by intermediaries—shopkeepers, wholesalers, shippers and more. The Internet is linking strangers living thousands of miles apart yet who can see and talk to each other. The Industrial Revolution in the simple mechanics of the eighteenth century is being surpassed by the transformed supply and demand of the magnified Market Revolution that began in the late twentieth century and will grow exponentially in the twenty-first.

Not least, the notions among scholars, from economists to scientists, on the power of ideas over human action will have to change. The brightest intelligences teach that intellectuals can initiate political change. Politicians will have to accept with humility that their years of dominating human life are passing.

Means of Escape

One of the most recent developments is the exertion of market forces in humble family life to avoid, by escaping from, the politically determined inadequate financing of state education. Parents of children at state schools, ambitious for their future in the age of the computer, are not content with accepting the inadequate financing and technical equipment of the state schools. They not only increasingly pay fees. They also, after school hours, pay private tutors to teach their children the use of personal computers to ensure they are not handicapped in their later higher education opportunities and employment prospects.

The new British Prime Minister was coached to anticipate the coming technological revolution and early spoke of the guiding principle of his government to be "Education, Education, Education." He announced his arrangement with a leading technological company to equip all 25,000 state schools with "free" computers—that is, without direct charge to parents. He did not mention their indirect payments by taxes, or their opportunity costs, for example by a host of delayed road improvements. The government-private enterprise compact will not be able to keep pace with the rate of advance and sophisticated variety of the new flood of innovations that the market will produce in the twenty-first century.

The intention of parents to better the prospects of their children will accelerate the long lead of the private schools over the state schools in teaching and equipping pupils for lives of work and fulfilment.

The extreme political outcome may be the demand of the egalitarian conscience that such "offensive inequalities" be suppressed by government prohibition and regulation. The political process will be urged on by the rent seeking outlined by Professor Tullock and illustrated by Dr. Brady for North America. In Britain rent seeking has long been exerted by the teacher trade unions, made powerful because the state has largely confined schooling to the state schools. But it will now lag behind the growing determination of parents with rising incomes to better the opportunities of their children for their lifetimes by making the best of their qualities.

In the larger canvas of the welfare state, not only in education, and not only between individual or groups of Members of Parliament, the two main political parties have in recent decades rolled each other's logs. With varying reluctance, and opposition from groups with long-term strategic outlooks rather than short-term tactical aims, the two main political parties have continued each other's policies. They have both overlooked the new powers of the people to escape from policies outdated by economic advance.

Government or Anarchy: Posing a False Choice

For three centuries thinking on the optimum role for government has been dominated by the belief, or fear, sown by Thomas Hobbes—that the alternative was anarchic chaos. That was not the alternative or the choice. The alternatives were not government or no government but too little or too much government. And for a century economists have attempted to define the boundary of acceptable government—neither too little nor too much—by analysing the extent of "public goods." The error, restated by the new British Minister of Social Services, Alastair Darling, was to suppose that government would not only supply them efficiently but that it would also withdraw from them as soon as they could be supplied by a choice of suppliers catering for individuals or families or small private groups with varying tastes.

This is the apotheosis of permanent politicised state welfare. It was the development of public choice which revealed the defects of collective supply and demand by government—the political process in which choices were expressed by the people with few choices as voters every few years rather than as consumers with numerous choices every day.

Thomas Hobbes, the seventeenth-century philosopher, in his notorious book *Leviathan*[2] (1650), confused thought on the nature of government that could ensure liberty and at the same time gave a powerful weapon to the advocates of big government down the centuries. Without "sovereignty," he said, by which he meant strong government by the state, there would be chaos and anarchy.

But that was over three centuries ago. In the twenty-first century, political power will have to be exercised with more reticence and more respect for the common people. It will have to be used in deference to the sentiments of the populace who will have new powers to challenge the state. If government, as it now does, uses its powers to enact laws, rules, regulations and other commands that flout the sentiments of the people it will find they can escape as they never could before.

The 300-year-old warning of Hobbes, in a very different world, does not validate the excesses of collective "public choice" that offend the real personal "choices" of the real sovereign public in the new world of the twenty-first century.

2. Thomas Hobbes, *Leviathan* (1650), Everyman's Library, London: J. M. Dent & Sons, 1924.

ON THE LIBERAL EMANCIPATION OF MANKIND

On the Liberal Emancipation of Mankind

Introduction

When some years ago Christian Watrin asked me to talk to his students my opening words in German seemed to surprise them. When we exchanged views about economic policies their fluent English surprised me. The German students were better linguists than the British; and I recognized in their teacher a worthy descendent of the German pre-war and post-war classical liberal economists.

In the twenty-first century economists of the classical liberal school will pass from studying what government should do to what it can do.

The question asked by Eugen von Böhm-Bawerk, "Macht oder Ökonomisches Gesetz" in 1914, best translated into "Political Power or Economic Law?," had to wait until the last decade of the twentieth century for the decisive answer.

The acceleration in technological invention in the 1990s has finally answered Böhm-Bawerk's question. In the twenty-first century, probably in the first two decades, 2000 to 2020, the escapes from superfluous government that has inhibited individual freedom and perpetuated poverty will have shrunken political control of economic life from 40% in Europe and North America, to 10%. Escape by the internet is a foregone conclusion. No single country, however large, or federal union, or continent, will be able to prevent its private citizens or adventurous entrepreneurs from trading with one another without political impediments. The lessons and warnings of the public choice school against the tolerance of political power have been learned too slowly. The long-outdated expansion of government is now ending. It has been expanded too soon without allowing the market to demonstrate its potential, expanded too far beyond the sphere of public goods, and continued too long after its plausible boundaries have been long exceeded. And it is now retreating too slowly before the compelling evidence that it is inferior to the mounting superiority of the market.

Its inevitable fate is to be abandoned through increasing escapes. The most fundamental is through rising incomes that enable more voters to replace its inferior schools, medicine, housing, pensions and insurance, its roads, transport and fuel, and to reject its low morals and high taxes. A little-noticed escape is through barter in the full range of private exchange from personal services to industrial swapping of surpluses of spare parts. Not the least escape that is growing imperceptibly is the parallel economy that is falsifying most of the official government statistics of national income, national output, the "social" statistics of poverty and inequality, the employment statistics of registered unemployment and the financial statistics of savings, investment, borrowings and prices.

The Failing Fiscal Sympathy

Taxes are best levied when government and people share the view that they are likely to be used to benefit the taxpayers: This shared sentiment has been weakened in Europe—and other continents—in recent decades. The recent growth of the "parallel" economy especially in Europe but also around the world is evidence of the weakening sympathy between governments and peoples. In Britain the deteriorating quality of state education, the "National" Health "Service" and other tax-financed industries has raised the question, long emphasized by liberal economists, whether these and other activities should ever have been provided by the state. The task is to identify whether the prime offender is the tax-payer for rejecting the poor quality of state services, or the state for demanding payment for services that deny choice by widely differing individuals and families and the freedom to escape to better services offered by markets in welfare, transport, fuel and "public" amenities.

Economic Liberals and Europe

Christian Watrin shares the anxieties of other classical liberals on the uncertainties and risks of progressively federalizing the sovereign states of Europe. Not least is the necessity of regional flexibility to accommodate agreed exchange rates.

Two potential advantages may receive less attention. Other federal unions—in the USA, Canada, Australia (and in Europe, Italy and Germany)—have reaped the economies of specialization facilitated by the abandonment of state obstruction to trade between the federated states. Low incomes, even much poverty, lingers longer in continents with largely sovereign nation states.

The other potential advantage is the earlier warnings, or evidence, of potential "illiberal" national tendencies that conflict with the general shared liberal sentiments of nations that have accepted a degree of federal identity. The emergence of illiberal tendencies in the early 1930s in Germany was not detected in time to strengthen the liberal elements. In the European Union there is early opportunity to detect illiberal national tendencies that may conflict with the underlying liberal principles of the union.

Little wonder that state taxes are being rejected, its regulations bypassed, its rules flouted. If "democracy" has been weakened, the reason is that "democratic" politicians have abused their powers to act as benefactors.

The Historic Delusion

Talk of "the retreat of the state" creates apprehension among the many who have regarded it as the saviour of the sick and the poor. A dominant anxiety is that democracy has taught the doctrine of Thomas Hobbes that its creation of "sovereignty" (government power over economic life) is essential for the maintenance of good order and civilized life. The alternative to the political state with the power to regulate economic life and to coerce the people to conform to it, warned Hobbes, was "a state of nature" that would create perpetual "war of all against all" in which life would be "nasty, brutish and short." This dire prospect has habituated the Western world into accepting and tolerating the political state with its over-government. Yet from the start of the twentieth century, or earlier, over-government has been an obstruction to the liberties that democracy was supposed to protect.

Hobbes wrote in the seventeenth century. His warning has long been overtaken by the technological advances of the nineteenth century with its massive rises in living standards. A century after Hobbes, at the end of the eighteenth century, it was still plausible for Thomas Paine to urge, in his classic *The Rights of Man,* an early structure of Beveridge Plan benefits from maternity grants through a form of school vouchers all the way to funeral expenses. In the introduction to the 1958 edition of *The Rights of Man* I wrote of Paine's proposals:

> In his day this was advanced thinking. In our day we have no sooner erected a structure of state provision for the needy than it has become out of date with rising personal incomes. The welfare state is, or in a free

> society should be, a passing phase; but there is a danger that it will be erected into a permanent appendage: the crutch will be beaten into a shackle.

So it has been for forty years since 1958, and indeed for over a century and a half. The recent reforms in the welfare state provoke a reassessment of Hobbes' flawed warning. It was rejected by the inter-war scholar, A. D. Lindsay, the Master of Balliol College, Oxford, in his introduction to Hobbes' *Leviathan.* Law is not obeyed solely because it is created by the state; it is respected essentially because it is wanted by the people. This truth is still overlooked by the politicians of our day. A. D. Lindsay stated:

> if Hobbes is right in maintaining that without some authority there can be no state . . . he forgets that the power of the sovereign, even though legally unlimited, depends upon the skill with which it gives expression to the general will; if it disregards the general will there will come a point at which *no amount of legal or constitutional machinery will avert disaster.* [My emphasis.]

The legal and constitutional machinery of the twentieth century has not prevented the emerging revolt of the masses.

Hobbes was earlier refuted by the seventeenth-century philosopher, Benedict de Spinoza. Lindsay repeats Spinoza's magisterial dictum:

> A sovereign has right insofar as he has might, and he has might only insofar as he rules in such a way that his subjects regard rebellion as a greater evil than obedience.

The sovereign state is now having to retreat from social welfare and other superfluous functions. But it is retreating too slowly. The subjects are rebelling. And they will continue to rebel until government retreats sufficiently to liberate the freedoms created by economic advance.

INDEX

The text for this book is set in Minion; the display type is Meta Plus Book. Both are relatively new faces, chosen to reflect Seldon's influence on and activity in contemporary social and economic thought. Minion was designed by Robert Slimbach for Adobe in 1990. In spirit and intent it derives from the Garamond tradition. Meta, designed by Erik Spiekermann in 1993, with open spacing for legibility at small sizes, has grown into an extended family and is now widely used.

Printed on paper that is acid-free and meets the requirements of the American National Standard for Permanence of Paper for Printed Library Materials, z39.48-1992. ♾

Book design by Barbara Williams, BW&A Books, Inc., Durham, North Carolina
Typography by Graphic Composition, Inc., Athens, Georgia
Printed and bound by Edwards Brothers, Inc., Ann Arbor, Michigan